A MODERN GUIDE TO HOMESTEADING

Accessible Strategies and Creative Ideas for Livestock Care, Homestead Equipment, Garden Setup, Sustainable Energy, and Self-Sufficient Living in Your Community.

Homestead Mentors

TABLE OF CONTENTS

INTRODUCTION

When we first traded our little town's constant hum for the quiet of our 10-acre homestead, it felt like stepping into a storybook. There we were, my husband and I, standing on our front porch with our 6-month-old little boy, with nothing but the wind to keep us company. It was exhilarating and terrifying all at once. The town had its comforts and predictability, but out here, we were greeted with challenges unknown. The chickens didn't care about our schedules, and the garden didn't wait for us to catch up on our reading. Yet, with every sunrise, these challenges turned into unexpected joys. The kind that can't be boxed or bought. The kind that fills your heart with a quiet contentment.

This book, "A Modern Guide to Homesteading," is born from those experiences. Its purpose is simple: to serve as a guide for anyone yearning to embrace sustainable living. Whether you're on a sprawling farm or a tiny urban plot, this book offers practical, adaptable solutions to help you make the most of what you have. It's about empowering you to live a life that aligns with your values and aspirations.

Who is this book for? It's for those who dream of harvesting food, crafting with their hands, and nurturing their connection to the earth. It's for urban dwellers with a small garden, DIY enthusiasts craving projects, and families wanting to slow down and simplify. It's for anyone who looks at a piece of land, no matter its size, and sees potential. This guide welcomes everyone, from seasoned homesteaders to those just dipping their toes into this lifestyle.

The themes we explore together are as diverse as the readers themselves. We'll talk about self-sufficiency and finding ways to produce what you need. We'll delve into adaptability, teaching you to tailor solutions to your unique circumstances. Health and wellness will be a core focus as we examine the benefits of homegrown food and natural products.

Community building is another cornerstone. You'll discover ways to connect with others who share your passion, creating a supportive and knowledge-sharing network. We'll weave modern innovations with traditional practices, showing you how to embrace technology while honoring time-tested methods.

This book stands out through a focus on flexibility and innovation. You'll find solutions here if you're dealing with limited space, a tight budget, or a challenging climate. We integrate modern technologies like renewable energy and innovative tools, showing how they can enhance traditional homesteading without overshadowing it.

From Dreams to Reality: My Homesteading Journey

Let me take a moment to share my story. I'm Ashley, a devoted wife, proud mom to two amazing boys, a full-time employee, and the founder of Homestead Mentors. Life on the homestead began as a leap of faith for my family and me, transitioning from the familiar comforts of town life to the raw beauty and challenges of rural living. What started as a dream of a simpler, more sustainable life turned into a journey of discovery, perseverance, and profound growth.

Through trial and error, I learned the rhythms of homestead-ing-from planting a garden and raising animals to preserving food and embracing a self-sufficient lifestyle. Along the way, I realized that this journey wasn't just about learning new skills.

Introduction

It was also about reconnecting with God's creation, fostering resilience, and finding joy in everyday moments.

My mission with Homestead Mentors is simple: to inspire, educate, and support those who feel called to craft a life that aligns with their values and dreams. Whether you're just starting to explore the idea of homesteading or you're ready to dig deeper into the lifestyle, I'm here to walk alongside you, offering encouragement, practical advice, and a sense of community.

This book is an extension of that mission. It is organized to guide you step-by-step, starting with the basics and laying the foundation of homesteading principles. From there, each chapter builds on the last, introducing more advanced techniques and ideas. By the end, you'll understand how to integrate these practices into your daily life.

You'll find actionable insights and personal stories woven throughout as you read. Each project or idea is designed to be practical, encouraging you to roll up your sleeves and get started. You'll find the information you can implement right away, whether you're setting up a small garden or planning a larger project.

Let's embark on this journey together. Homesteading has the power to transform your life. It fosters independence and resilience. It deepens your connection to the world around you. Most importantly, it offers a sense of fulfillment and peace that is truly priceless.

Welcome to a life of intention and abundance. Welcome to your homesteading journey.

1

LAYING THE GROUNDWORK FOR HOMESTEADING SUCCESS

When we first moved to our homestead, there was a moment I'll never forget. I was standing in the middle of our new yard, boots sinking into the earth, feeling both thrilled and utterly overwhelmed. The land was vast, a canvas of possibility, but it was also a blank slate without the cozy confines of town life. This was no small feat. It was a leap into a new world. Yet, with each sunrise, the land whispered its secrets, and slowly, I learned to listen. Those early days taught me the importance of having a clear vision of what I wanted to achieve and a roadmap to guide me through the unknown. I realized that before any seeds were planted or chickens were tended, a solid foundation needed to be laid. This chapter is about crafting that foundation-your homesteading vision.

1.1 Defining Your Homesteading Vision

Creating a personal vision statement is like drawing a map for your homesteading adventure. It's about capturing your motivations and dreams and setting a clear path forward. Start by asking yourself what values matter most to you. Is it sustainability? Self-sufficiency? Perhaps it's the joy of growing your own food or the thrill of building with your own hands. Whatever it is, let these values guide you. Write them down. Let them be your compass. Your vision statement should align with these values and paint a picture of the lifestyle you hope to cultivate. It might be a few sentences or a paragraph that resonates with you deeply. Keep it where you can see it-on your fridge or in your planner. Let it be a reminder of the "why" behind your homesteading efforts.

Here's our vision at Homestead Mentors:

Our homesteading journey is rooted in simplicity, connection, and purpose. We cherish the ability to step into our garden and gather fresh food as if we're shopping in nature's own grocery store. It's vital for us to teach our boys not only where their food comes from but also how to respect and care for the animals that share this land with us.

Building our own shelters, fences, and projects isn't just practical-it's therapeutic. These moments are where we find peace, creativity, and the joy of working side by side as a family. Sharing these experiences with friends, family, and our community brings us so much fulfillment.

Our farm is more than a home; it's a space for learning, growth, and connection. We believe life is short and precious and meant to be filled with what truly matters. By sharing our land, knowledge, and passion, we hope to inspire others to live with intention, gratitude, and abundance.

This vision is our compass, reminding us daily why we chose this path and encouraging us to share its beauty with those around us.

So, if we were to sum this up into a simple vision statement, it would look something like the following –

"Our homesteading vision is to create a space where our family and community can connect with the land, grow fresh food, build with purpose, and share meaningful experiences-living each day with intention, gratitude, and abundance."

Once you have your vision, the next step is to assess your resources and limitations. This means taking a good look at what you have to work with. Measure your space, whether it's a backyard, a patch of land, or even a balcony. Consider the time you can realistically dedicate to your homestead. Are you balancing a full-time job or other commitments? Be honest about your budget. Financial planning is crucial. Establishing a budget helps you prioritize what needs to be done now and what can wait. Think about the initial setup costs, like tools, seeds, and animals. Perhaps you might need fencing or a new coop. (See Source 2 for tips on financial planning.) Knowing your limitations isn't about discouraging yourself-it's about setting realistic expectations so you can plan effectively.

With your vision and resources in mind, it's time to set goals. This is where the dream takes shape in actionable steps. Break down your overarching vision into short-term and long term goals. Short-term goals might include starting a small vegetable garden or building a compost bin. Long-term goals, like becoming fully self-sufficient or starting a community garden, could be more ambitious. Develop a five-year plan that outlines these goals.

Consider what you'd like to achieve each year and map out the steps needed to get there. This plan serves as a roadmap, offering direction and motivation as you make progress.

Finally, cultivate a growth mindset. Homesteading is a journey filled with learning curves and unexpected twists. Embrace the changes and challenges that come your way, as they are opportunities for growth. Don't be afraid of failure. Every setback is a lesson, teaching you what works and what doesn't. Celebrate your successes, no matter how small, and use them to fuel your passion. Adaptability is key. As you grow and change, so too will your homesteading practices. Allow yourself the freedom to pivot and evolve.

When we first started our homestead, determining the best type of enclosures for our animals proved challenging. Initially, we built wooden pens for our goats, thinking they would be sturdy and cost-effective. However, as our farm grew to include larger animals like cows and horses, we discovered that wood deteriorated too quickly under their weight and the harsh Wyoming weather. This led us to replace the wooden structures with oil pipe pens, which have proven far more durable and suitable for our needs.

While adapting our animal pens was our main focus, similar challenges arose with our dairy cow milking stanchion and water systems. Each required iterations and adjustments, like eventually moving to an automatic watering system that doesn't freeze in winter, drastically simplifying our daily chores.

These experiences highlighted the constant need for adaptation in homesteading, ensuring that our practices best meet the evolving needs of our farm and animals. Each of these challenges shaped us. They taught us resilience, patience, and the value of adapting when something isn't working. Homesteading isn't about having it all figured out from the start- it's about being willing to learn, pivot, and grow with every obstacle that comes your way.

Consider creating a vision board or journal where you can collect inspiration, ideas, and reflections. This can be a powerful tool for keeping your vision alive and tangible. (See Source 1 for more on using vision statements.) As you embark on your homesteading journey, remember that it's not about perfection. It's about progress, exploration, and meaningful connections with the land.

1.2 Understanding Self-Sufficiency in Modern Times

When people hear "self-sufficiency," they often picture a lone cabin in the woods, someone living off the grid, completely detached from society. But in today's world, self-sufficiency is much more nuanced. It's about finding a harmony between being self-reliant and engaging with the community around you. Imagine a neighborhood where everyone grows different vegetables and shares the bounty with each other. That's a glimpse into modern self-sufficiency. It's less about isolating oneself and more about building networks that reduce our dependency on large, impersonal systems. By sharing skills and resources, we foster a supportive community while gaining the satisfaction of contributing in tangible ways.

The benefits of pursuing a self-sufficient lifestyle are manifold. For starters, you'll find yourself less reliant on commercial systems, which can be erratic and impersonal. Growing your own food, for instance, means fewer trips to the store, less exposure to supply chain disruptions, and the joy of eating produce you've nurtured from seed to table. It's empowering to know that you can meet many of your own needs. This lifestyle also enhances personal resilience. When you learn to fix things yourself, troubleshoot problems, and adapt to changing circumstances, you build a toolkit of skills that serve you well in all areas of life. These abilities are invaluable, especially in uncertain times, offering a sense of security and independence.

However, it's important to approach self-sufficiency with realistic expectations. One common misconception is the belief in complete independence as if true self-sufficiency means cutting all ties with the outside world. This isn't just impractical; it's nearly impossible in modern society. We all rely on each other in ways we might not initially realize. Another myth is the notion that self-sufficiency requires less time and effort than traditional living. In reality, it demands a significant investment of both. Whether you're building a greenhouse or learning to preserve food, these tasks take time to master. Yet, the rewards, both tangible and intangible, are well worth the effort.

To ease into self-sufficiency, start with small, manageable projects. Perhaps begin with a windowsill herb garden or a backyard compost pile. These projects don't require much space or resources, but they offer a taste of what's possible. From there, gradually expand your efforts, maybe by planting a vegetable garden or learning to make your own soap.

Remember, you don't have to go on this journey alone. At Homestead Mentors, we've created a welcoming online space where like-minded individuals can share their experiences, ask questions, and celebrate milestones together. Join our community at **homesteadmentors.com** or connect with us on Facebook at **facebook.com/homesteadmentors.** Whether you're just starting out or have years of experience, you'll find inspiration, support, and practical advice from a network of fellow homesteaders. Together, we can grow, learn, and thrive!

Exploring multiple forums and communities, especially those specific to your region, is important. Local groups can offer valuable insight into climate-specific challenges, regional resources, and nearby suppliers. Whether you're connecting online or attending local workshops, building a diverse support network will equip you with knowledge, encouragement, and a sense of belonging.

By taking these steps, you'll find that self-sufficiency isn't about going it alone. It's about creating a life that reflects your values, with a community that supports and enriches your efforts. You'll experience the satisfaction of knowing that you can provide for yourself in meaningful ways, while still enjoying the camaraderie and collaboration of others who are on a similar path.

On our farm, we've had the joy of welcoming families to learn hands-on skills like processing meat birds, milking goats and cows, and harvesting fresh produce. Neighbors, friends, and family have joined us in the garden to share the harvest and learn how to preserve food for the winter months. We've also hosted community dinners with like minded friends. These gatherings are filled with meaningful conversation, brainstorming ways to strengthen our homesteads and support one another in our shared goals. This balance of self-reliance and community connection is what makes self-sufficiency in modern times not only achievable but deeply rewarding.

Take some time to reflect on what self-sufficiency means to you. Consider the following questions:

- What are some areas of your life where you would like to be more self-reliant?
- How can you integrate community support into your self-sufficiency goals?
- What small project can you start today that moves you toward greater independence?

As you reflect on these questions, we want to share how we're currently answering them on our own homestead:

Right now, we're planning to expand our barn. This extra space will serve multiple purposes-from storing more food and hosting larger farm events, to offering living quarters for visiting friends and family, and even generating extra income by renting out the living space on platforms like Airbnb.

We've been reaching out to our network, asking what resources they might know to help us approach this project in the most affordable and efficient way. Our community is full of talented individuals-plumbers, concrete experts, and skilled handymen-who generously offer advice and assistance.

This isn't a small project; we know it may take over a year to complete. But we're continuously asking ourselves how we can grow and improve our homestead to leave a legacy for the next generation.

Like us, your answers to these questions might involve big dreams and small, actionable steps. No matter how small, every effort brings you closer to greater self-sufficiency.

Write down your thoughts and revisit them as you continue your homesteading journey. This reflection can serve as a guiding light, helping you stay focused on the aspects of self-sufficiency that matter most to you.

1.3 Balancing Technology with Traditional Practices

In our fast-paced world, technology is like a double-edged sword. On the one hand, it offers amazing tools that can simplify our lives; on the other, it can be overwhelming, threatening to overshadow the timeless practices that have served us well for generations. Finding the right balance between these two is key to creating a homestead that's both efficient and soulful.

Start by evaluating which technological tools can truly complement your efforts without taking the joy out of the process. For instance, a smart gardening app can be a handy assistant, offering reminders about watering schedules, plant care tips, and even identifying pests or diseases with a quick photo. These apps can make managing a garden more intuitive, allowing you to focus on the hands-on work that brought you to homesteading in the first place.

Solar-powered devices also bring a modern edge to traditional practices. From solar lights that illuminate your pathways to solar water pumps that keep your garden lush, or fences that keep your animals safe, these devices harness renewable energy to power your homestead. They're environmentally friendly and reduce dependency on external power sources. The key is to use technology as a tool to enhance your homesteading experience, not replace it. Choose devices that align with your values and will genuinely make your tasks easier or more enjoyable. It's about complementing the tactile, earthy experiences with smart solutions that save time and energy.

Traditional methods, meanwhile, form the heart of home-steading. Practices like companion planting have been passed down through generations for good reason. By planting certain species together, you can enhance growth, naturally repel pests, and optimize space. It's an art and science that respects the rhythms of nature, and it's incredibly rewarding to see the harmony in your garden. Similarly, tried-and-true animal husbandry practices ensure that your livestock is healthy and productive. These methods are rooted in a deep understanding of animal behavior and welfare, drawing on the wisdom of those who have walked this path before us.

Finding a balance between technology and tradition involves a blend of innovation and reverence for the past. Consider the example of small-scale farmers who integrate GPS technology for precision farming while still employing crop rotation techniques that date back centuries. This hybrid approach maximizes yield and sustainability, demonstrating how modern tools and ancestral knowledge can work hand in hand. Adaptability is crucial. As the world changes, so must our approaches. Embrace new innovations that align with your goals yet remain rooted in the practices that resonate with you. This combination creates a dynamic, resilient homestead that honors both past and present.

Modern machinery and equipment can also play a significant role, depending on the size of your homestead. For those with more expansive land, tillage and land-clearing equipment can be invaluable, preparing the soil efficiently for planting larger crops. On smaller plots, more compact agricultural equipment may suffice, allowing you to work the land without overwhelming it. Choose machinery that matches your scale and needs, ensuring it supports rather than dominates your homesteading activities. The right tools can make tasks more manageable, freeing up time and energy for other pursuits.

On our homestead, two pieces of equipment have been absolute game-changers: our tractor and our chicken plucker.

Our tractor, equipped with a cab and air conditioning, was a significant investment and one we carefully considered. With a monthly payment of about $400 and a no-interest loan, we'll have it fully paid off in three years. But already, it has proven to be worth every penny. The tractor allows us to hay our own acreage, which provides feed for our animals and even helps neighboring farms hay their fields, offsetting the cost of ownership. In the snowy Wyoming winters, it clears our driveway, ensuring we can get vehicles in and out safely. It also simplifies cleaning animal pens, and on lighter days, provides joyful hayrides for birthday parties. Even with our 10-acre farm, the tractor has been an investment that pays for itself year after year.

Another essential tool we can't live without is our chicken plucker. Raising and processing meat birds is an important part of our homestead, and hand-plucking chickens is not only time-consuming but also incredibly tedious. Our chicken plucker has saved us hundreds of hours during processing season, freeing up time for other essential tasks. It's one of those smaller investments that delivers big returns in saved time and energy.

These tools have been carefully chosen based on our homestead's specific needs, and they've allowed us to work smarter, not harder. When selecting machinery, always consider how it will fit into your day-to-day tasks and whether it will pay for itself in time, efficiency, or income generation.

Adaptability applies to technology and environmental changes as well. With the climate in flux, being able to adjust your methods is more important than ever. This might mean shifting planting schedules, trying new crop varieties, or implementing water-saving techniques. It's about staying observant and responsive, using both technology and traditional knowledge to navigate challenges and seize opportunities. Embracing change doesn't mean abandoning what works; it's about integrating new insights in a way that enriches your homestead.

A successful balance between technology and tradition is a personal endeavor. It's about what feels right for you and what resonates with your values and vision. As you explore this balance, remember that there's no one-size-fits-all solution. What works for one homestead might not work for another. The journey is about finding what makes you feel connected, empowered, and inspired. This balance, like a well-tended garden, requires patience, attention, and a willingness to learn and adapt. And in this dance between the new and the old, you'll craft a homestead that's uniquely yours, one that thrives in harmony with both the tools of today and the wisdom of yesterday.

1.4 Creating a Seasonal Project Calendar

When I first began homesteading, I quickly learned that nature runs on its own schedule. The rhythm of the seasons dictates when to plant, when to harvest, and when to let the land rest. Understanding this natural rhythm is crucial for maximizing efficiency and productivity on your homestead. A carefully crafted seasonal project calendar can become your guiding star. It aligns your activities with these natural cycles, ensuring that you're making the most of each season's unique opportunities. This approach not only boosts productivity but also reduces the stress of trying to do everything at once. By breaking down tasks according to the season, you can focus your energy where it matters most, letting nature's timeline lead the way.

Creating a personalized calendar tailored to your specific climate and personal goals is the next step. Begin by researching the peak planting and harvest times for your region. This information might come from local gardening clubs, agricultural extensions, or even neighbors who have been tending their gardens for years. Once you know when your growing season begins and ends, you can plan accordingly.

Here's the garden planner we use every year to help us on the homestead: https://www.homesteadmentors.com/offers/YvfuzjdW

[Scan QR Code]

Mark these times on your calendar and then consider what maintenance tasks need to be scheduled regularly. Perhaps it's feeding the chickens or rotating crops. By having these tasks mapped out, you'll avoid the last-minute scrambles that can make homesteading feel overwhelming. This planning helps ensure that each task is completed at the right time, maximizing efficiency and reducing unnecessary stress.

Flexibility is key to any successful plan, and your calendar should be no different. Weather can be unpredictable, and unexpected events can throw even the best-laid plans off course. Build flexibility into your calendar by creating contingency plans for potential disruptions.

For example, if a late frost is forecasted, know how you will protect your plants. If a dry spell hits, have a backup plan for water conservation. Being prepared for the unexpected allows you to adapt quickly, keeping your homestead running smoothly despite any hiccups. Flexibility doesn't mean you abandon your schedule-it means you're ready to adjust it as needed, maintaining progress without feeling derailed.

Regularly reviewing and adjusting your calendar is vital in keeping it relevant and effective. Monthly or quarterly reviews can help you assess what's working and what needs tweaking. This process allows you to reflect on past experiences, learning from them to improve future plans. Perhaps you underestimated the time needed for pruning or found that a specific crop didn't thrive in your soil. Use these insights to refine your schedule, ensuring it remains a valuable tool rather than a rigid list of tasks. The more you engage with your calendar, the more it becomes a living document, evolving with you and your homestead.

To keep things interesting, consider adding a visual element to your calendar, like color-coding tasks by priority or type. This not only makes it easier to read at a glance but also adds a layer of creativity and personalization. You might use green for planting, blue for watering, and yellow for maintenance, creating a visual map of your homestead's needs. A visual calendar can serve as both a practical tool and a source of inspiration, reminding you of the vibrant, dynamic life you're cultivating.

Example below:

Month	Tasks	Priority	Category	Notes	Color Code
January	Plan garden layout, order seeds	High	Planning	Order seeds early to avoid delays	Green
February	Start seeds indoors	High	Planting	Use grow lights for indoor seeds	Green

March	Prepare soil, plant cold-hardy crops	Medium	Soil Preparation	Test soil pH and adjust	Brown
April	Plant main garden crops	High	Planting	Ensure proper spacing for crops	Green
May	Maintain garden, weed control	Medium	Maintenance	Check irrigation systems	Yellow
June	Harvest early crops, maintain watering	Medium	Harvesting	Monitor pests and diseases	Blue
July	Harvest summer crops, preserve produce	High	Harvesting	Start canning and preserving	Blue
August	Start fall planting, maintain compost	Medium	Planting	Prepare compost bins	Brown
September	Harvest fall crops, prepare for winter	High	Harvesting	Store harvested produce	Blue
October	Clean tools, prepare garden beds	Low	Maintenance	Sharpen tools and organize storage	Yellow
November	Maintain livestock, plan next year	Medium	Livestock	Evaluate animal feed stock	Orange
December	Reflect on year, plan improvements	Low	Planning	Set goals for next season	Orange

At its core, a seasonal project calendar is about aligning your efforts with the natural world, ensuring that you work with, and not against, the environment. It's a tool that brings clarity and purpose to your homesteading efforts, allowing you to focus on what truly matters. With a well-organized calendar, you can approach each day with confidence, knowing that your tasks are part of a larger, well-thought-out plan. This foresight transforms the chaos of daily chores into a harmonious symphony of activity, where each note contributes to the overall success of your homestead.

As you embark on crafting your own seasonal project calendar, remember that this is a process of discovery and adjustment. Embrace the learning curve and relish the satisfaction that comes from aligning your homestead with the changing seasons. This calendar isn't just about planning; it's about creating a lifestyle that respects and celebrates the natural cycles of the earth. By doing so, you cultivate not only a productive homestead but also a fulfilling, intentional way of living that brings joy and balance to your days.

2

DESIGNING YOUR SPACE
FOR MAXIMUM YIELD

The notion of transforming limited spaces into lush, productive gardens might seem daunting at first glance, especially when you're in an urban environment with little room to spare. Yet, it's precisely in these constraints where creativity flourishes. Discover effective gardening and beekeeping strategies that maximize yield and sustainability in small urban spaces in this chapter.

My friend had a tiny apartment balcony-barely large enough for a small table and I remember how she stared at the space, wondering how she could possibly grow anything meaningful there. At first, it felt impossible to cultivate more than a few potted plants. But then she discovered vertical gardening-a technique that not only maximizes space but also adds a vibrant aesthetic appeal to even the most compact areas.

Vertical gardening is a concept that flips traditional gardening on its head-quite literally. Instead of planting across the ground, you grow upwards, using walls, fences, and trellises as your canvas. This method is especially advantageous in cramped urban settings where horizontal space is a luxury. By utilizing vertical space, you can increase your yield without expanding your footprint. Not only does it save space, but it also creates an eye-catching display that can transform an ordinary wall into a living work of art. The convenience of having plants at eye level means easier access for maintenance and harvesting, reducing the need to bend over repeatedly. Vertical gardens also improve air circulation around plants, aiding in pest and disease management.

Choosing the right plants for vertical gardening is essential for success. You'll want to select varieties that thrive in elevated environments. Herbs such as mint, basil, and parsley are excellent choices due to their compact growth habits and frequent culinary use. Leafy greens like lettuce, spinach, and kale also perform well, providing a continuous harvest of fresh produce. Strawberries are a delightful addition, their trailing vines cascading down the garden structure, producing sweet fruit throughout the season. When selecting plants, consider their light requirements, growth patterns, and how they might benefit from being in a vertical setup. Avoid planting species together that compete for resources or are susceptible to similar diseases, such as tomatoes with strawberries.

Building a vertical garden structure is a rewarding DIY project that allows for plenty of personalization. One popular method involves using wooden pallets, which can often be sourced for free or at a low cost from local businesses. By attaching landscape fabric to the back and sides of a pallet, you create pockets for soil and plants. Once filled, the pallet can be leaned against a wall or fence, instantly transforming into a lush, green wall. Trellises are another fantastic option, particularly for climbing plants like beans and cucumbers. You can construct a simple trellis from bamboo poles or repurpose an old ladder to support vining plants. Wall planters, available in materials such as plastic, wood, or felt, offer a sleek alternative, allowing you to mount individual pots directly onto walls or fences. Each method provides an opportunity to tailor your garden to your space and aesthetic preferences.

Maintaining a vertical garden involves a few key practices to ensure the health and vitality of your plants. Watering can be a bit tricky in vertical setups, as gravity tends to pull moisture downward. To mitigate this, consider installing a drip irrigation system or using self-watering pots that help distribute water evenly. If you're hand-watering, be sure to reach the uppermost plants, as they tend to dry out more quickly. Regularly check for pests, as compact spaces can sometimes lead to faster spread if not monitored. Introduce beneficial insects like ladybugs to help manage potential infestations naturally. Vertical gardens also benefit from regular feeding, especially during peak growing seasons. Using a balanced, water-soluble fertilizer can provide the necessary nutrients to keep your plants thriving.

Take a moment to reflect on how a vertical garden could enhance your space. Consider these questions:

- What area in your home could be transformed into a vertical garden?
- Which plants do you use most often and would like to grow vertically?
- How can you incorporate elements of sustainability, such as repurposed materials, into your vertical garden design?

Write down your thoughts and ideas. This reflection can serve as a starting point for planning your own vertical garden, helping you visualize the possibilities and setting the stage for your urban oasis.

Rooftop Beekeeping: Harnessing the Heights

Imagine standing on a rooftop, surrounded not by the hustle and bustle of the city below but by the gentle hum of bees going about their work. Rooftop beekeeping offers urban homesteaders a unique opportunity to engage with nature in the most unexpected of places. By hosting beehives on rooftops, you not only contribute to the environmental health of your area through vital pollination but also enjoy the benefits of harvesting your own honey. Bees play an essential role in pollinating many of the plants we rely on for food, and by supporting them, you create a thriving ecosystem right above the city streets.

Furthermore, rooftop beekeeping provides an excellent way to produce honey, beeswax, and other bee-related products, turning an otherwise underutilized space into a productive hub.

Before setting up hives, it's important to consider the legal landscape and ensure that your rooftop meets safety standards. Every city has its own set of regulations governing urban beekeeping, which can include obtaining permits and adhering to specific guidelines for hive placement. It's a good idea to start by checking your local zoning laws to understand what's required. Some areas may require that hives be set back a certain distance from property lines, or that flyway barriers, such as fences or hedges, be installed to guide bees' flight paths upward and away from human activity. Ensuring safe access to the rooftop is also crucial, not only for regular hive maintenance but also for emergency situations. A well-constructed ladder or staircase, along with a secure rooftop surface, can make all the difference in providing safe and easy access.

When you're ready to set up your hives, consider the type of hive that will best suit your needs and the available space. Langstroth hives are a popular choice, known for their modular design and ease of management. They consist of stacked boxes, each containing frames where bees build their comb. Top-bar hives, on the other hand, offer a more natural approach, with bees constructing comb in a horizontal layout. These hives are often easier to inspect but may produce less honey. Positioning your hives to maximize sun exposure is key, as bees thrive in warmth and light. Additionally, placing hives where they're sheltered from strong winds can help maintain a stable environment, which is crucial for the bees' health and productivity.

Caring for bees in an urban setting presents unique challenges, but with the right techniques, you can maintain healthy and productive hives. Regular hive inspections are vital, especially as the seasons change. In spring, check for signs of growth and ensure the queen is laying eggs. Summer requires vigilant monitoring for pests and diseases, which can spread more easily in densely populated areas. In autumn, focus on preparing the hive for winter, ensuring there are enough food stores and that the hive is well-insulated. Urban environments may also expose bees to pollutants, so providing a clean water source close to the hives is essential. Bees use water to regulate the hive temperature and to dilute honey for feeding, so ensuring it's free of chemicals will support their health.

Managing urban-specific challenges means being adaptable and observant. Noise pollution, for instance, can sometimes stress bees, affecting their productivity. If your rooftop is near a busy street or construction site, consider adding sound barriers or positioning hives on the quieter side of the building. Additionally, urban heat islands can affect hive temperature, so monitoring and adjusting ventilation is critical. By keeping a close eye on your hives and responding to their needs, you create an environment where bees can thrive, contributing to the resilience and health of urban ecosystems. Through rooftop beekeeping, you not only connect with nature in a unique setting but also support the vital work of pollinators, ensuring a greener, more sustainable urban landscape.

2.3 Container Farming on a Budget

Container farming is a brilliant solution for those of us looking to grow fresh produce without the luxury of expansive land. Whether you're working with a small patio, a sunny corner of your apartment, or a modest backyard, containers can transform these spaces into fruitful gardens. The beauty of container farming lies in its flexibility and simplicity. You have the freedom to move containers around to catch the best light or protect them from harsh weather, giving you control over your plants' environment. This mobility is especially beneficial in urban areas where sunlight can be inconsistent. Moreover, container farming allows you to manage soil quality precisely, reducing the risks of pests and diseases that often plague traditional gardens. You can tailor the soil mix to suit each plant's needs, ensuring optimal growth conditions. This approach minimizes the guesswork and maximizes your gardening success, making it an ideal starting point for beginners.

When diving into container farming, choosing the right containers and soil is crucial. You don't need to spend a fortune on fancy pots; recycled containers work just as well. Think creatively-buckets, barrels, old bathtubs, or even tires can serve as excellent planting vessels. Just ensure they have proper drainage holes to prevent waterlogging, which can lead to root rot. For soil, opt for a high-quality potting mix, which is designed to provide the right balance of nutrients and drainage. You can enhance this mix with soil amendments like perlite or vermiculite to improve aeration and moisture retention. Compost is another fantastic addition, enriching the soil with organic matter that fosters healthy plant growth. The key is to maintain a balance that supports your plants' specific needs, whether they prefer drier or more moisture-retentive conditions.

Selecting the right plants can make all the difference in your container farming success, especially when working within a budget. Look for cost-effective options that promise high yields and fast growth. Radishes and lettuce are excellent choices, as they thrive in containers and mature quickly, allowing for multiple harvests in a single season. Perennial herbs like rosemary and thyme are another economical option, providing year-round flavor without the need for replanting. These plants not only save money but also offer the joy of having fresh, homegrown ingredients at your fingertips. When choosing plants, consider their light and space requirements to ensure your containers can accommodate their growth. Mixing and matching different plants in a single container can also add visual interest and maximize your harvest.

Here's a list of plant combinations that thrive in container gardens, complement each other, and maximize space and productivity:

1. **Tomatoes, Basil, and Marigolds**
   - ❏ *Why:* Tomatoes thrive with basil, which can improve their flavor, while marigolds deter pests.

2. **Lettuce, Radishes, and Carrots**
   - ❏ *Why:* These plants have different root depths and grow well together without competing for space.

3. **Peppers, Onions, and Oregano**
   - ❏ *Why:* Peppers and onions complement each other, and oregano helps deter pests.

4. **Strawberries, Spinach, and Chives**
   - ❏ *Why:* Strawberries grow upward while spinach and chives fill the lower space.

5. **Cucumbers, Dill, and Nasturtiums**
   - ❏ *Why:* Cucumbers climb, dill repels pests, and nasturtiums act as a natural pest deterrent.

6. **Kale, Swiss Chard, and Mint**
   - ❏ *Why:* These leafy greens coexist well, and mint helps deter pests naturally.

7. **Eggplant, Bush Beans, and Thyme**
   - ❏ *Why:* Bush beans fix nitrogen in the soil, benefiting eggplants, and thyme helps deter pests.

8. **Zucchini, Marigolds, and Basil**
   - ❏ *Why:* Zucchini needs space to sprawl, marigolds deter pests, and basil enhances growth.

9. **Snap Peas, Lettuce, and Dill**
   - ❏ *Why:* Peas grow upward, lettuce fills the lower layer, and dill attracts beneficial insects.

10. **Garlic, Lettuce, and Beets**
    - ❏ *Why:* Garlic repels pests, lettuce grows quickly, and beets use deeper soil levels.

Efficient watering and fertilization are vital to maintaining healthy container plants. Containers dry out faster than garden beds, so it's important to monitor moisture levels regularly. A simple DIY drip irrigation system can be a lifesaver, providing consistent water without the hassle of daily hand watering. You can create one using inexpensive materials like tubing and emitters, customizing it to fit your container layout. If manual watering is more your style, try watering in the early morning or late afternoon to minimize evaporation.

Along with watering, your plants will need regular feeding to thrive. Homemade organic fertilizers, such as compost tea or diluted fish emulsion, can provide essential nutrients without the chemicals found in commercial options. These homemade solutions are not only cost-effective but also environmentally friendly, aligning with a sustainable lifestyle. Adjust fertilization frequency based on plant growth stages, ramping up during peak growing periods and tapering off as plants mature.

Compost Tea Fertilizer

Why use it: Compost tea is a nutrient-rich liquid fertilizer that boosts plant health and improves soil structure.

Ingredients:

- 1 part well-aged compost
- 5 parts water
- A large bucket (5-gallon size works well)
- A stirring stick
- A strainer or cheesecloth

Instructions:

1. Fill a 5-gallon bucket with water (preferably rainwater or dechlorinated tap water).
2. Add one part of compost to the water. Stir well.
3. Let the mixture steep for 24-48 hours, stirring occasionally.
4. After steeping, strain the mixture using cheesecloth or a fine mesh strainer to remove solid particles.
5. Pour the liquid into a watering can or sprayer.

How to Use:

- Dilute the compost tea in a 1:1 ratio with water.
- Apply directly to the soil around your plants or spray lightly on leaves.
- Use every 1-2 weeks during the growing season.

Tip: Avoid using compost tea on edible leaves (like lettuce) close to harvest to minimize contamination risk.

Fish Emulsion Fertilizer

Why use it: Fish emulsion is an excellent all-purpose fertilizer, rich in nitrogen, phosphorus, and potassium, perfect for leafy greens and fruiting plants.

Ingredients:

- 1 part fish scraps (fish heads, guts, and bones)
- 2 parts water
- A large bucket with a tight-fitting lid
- A stirring stick

Instructions:

1. Place fish scraps in a bucket and add two parts water.
2. Seal the bucket with a lid to reduce odors.
3. Stir the mixture every 2-3 days for about 2 weeks.
4. Once the fish scraps have broken down and the water is dark, strain the mixture into a container.

How to Use:

- Dilute fish emulsion with water at a ratio of 1:4 (1 part fish emulsion to 4 parts water).
- Apply directly to the soil at the base of plants every 2-3 weeks.
- Avoid pouring on leaves to prevent burning.

Tip: Wear gloves and use this fertilizer outdoors-it can have a strong smell!

Container farming is a gateway to sustainable, self-sufficient living, allowing you to grow fresh produce regardless of space constraints. It's about making the most of what you have, using creativity and resourcefulness to cultivate a thriving garden. Whether you're growing a few herbs for your kitchen or a diverse array of vegetables, container farming offers a practical and rewarding approach to gardening that anyone can embrace. By starting small and expanding as your confidence grows, you'll find that container farming not only provides food but also fosters a deeper connection to the natural world, bringing the joys of gardening to any space.

2.4 Polyculture for Small Yards

Imagine stepping into a garden that mimics nature's ecosystem, with plants growing in harmony, supporting one another, and thriving together. This is the essence of polyculture. Unlike monoculture, which focuses on a single crop, polyculture involves cultivating multiple species in the same space. This approach maximizes biodiversity and yield, particularly in small yards where every square foot matters. The beauty of polyculture lies in its ability to enhance soil health and naturally control pests, reducing the need for chemical interventions. By fostering a diverse plant community, you create a resilient environment where plants complement and support each other, leading to abundant, varied harvests.

Designing a polyculture system begins with understanding your yard's unique conditions and selecting companion planting combinations that thrive together. Companion planting involves pairing plants that have beneficial relationships, such as deterring pests, attracting pollinators, or enhancing nutrient availability. For instance, marigolds planted alongside tomatoes can deter nematodes, while basil can improve tomato growth and flavor.

Staggered planting is another valuable strategy, where you plant crops at intervals to ensure a continuous harvest throughout the growing season. This not only optimizes space but also maintains soil fertility as different plants contribute and extract nutrients at varying rates.

When it comes to selecting and grouping plants for a successful polyculture, the Three Sisters planting method is a time-tested example. This Native American technique involves interplanting corn, beans, and squash. The corn provides a natural trellis for the climbing beans, which in turn fix nitrogen in the soil, benefiting all three crops. The squash's broad leaves act as a natural mulch, suppressing weeds and retaining soil moisture. Incorporating nitrogen-fixing plants such as clover or peas can further enrich your garden. These plants capture atmospheric nitrogen and convert it into a form usable by other plants, promoting robust growth without synthetic fertilizers.

Managing a polyculture garden requires some strategy but offers rewarding results. Rotational planting is a key practice, where you change the location of plant families each season to prevent disease buildup and nutrient depletion. This practice mimics natural succession, keeping your soil healthy and your plants vigorous. When it's time to harvest, mixed cropping presents its own set of techniques. For instance, you may need to carefully navigate beneath sprawling squash vines to access the beans climbing up the corn. This diversity can make harvesting a bit of a treasure hunt, but it also means you're less likely to face a total crop failure due to pests or disease. The varied growth patterns ensure that if one crop underperforms, others can fill the gap, providing food security and a dynamic, engaging gardening experience.

By embracing polyculture, you invite a bit of nature's complexity into your yard. This method not only enhances productivity but also enriches your experience as a gardener. You become a steward of a tiny ecosystem, observing the intricate interactions between plants and the insects and animals they attract. With each season, you'll gain insights into which combinations thrive in your specific conditions, allowing you to refine and expand your approach. In small yards, where space is precious, polyculture offers a way to make the most of every inch, turning your garden into a vibrant tapestry of life and growth.

Below are a couple of garden layouts for small yards. The Companion Planting Garden (10x10 feet)

Focus: Maximizing yield and natural pest control.

This layout groups plants that benefit each other by repelling pests, improving soil; or enhancing growth.

Layout Plan:

- **Front Row (South Side, Sunniest Spot)**
  - ❑ **Tomatoes (2 plants)** - Provide shade for smaller plants.
  - ❑ **Basil (4 plants)** - Enhances tomato flavor and repels pests.
- **Middle Row (Partial Shade from Tomatoes)**
  - ❑ **Lettuce (4 heads)** - Grows well in partial shade.
  - ❑ **Carrots (10 plants)** - Beneficial root crops that break up the soil.
- **Back Row (North Side, Taller Plants)**
  - ❑ **Pole Beans (4 plants, climbing trellis)** -Add nitrogen to the soil.
  - ❑ **Marigolds (2 plants)** - Repel pests and attract pollinators.

Key Benefits:

- Tomatoes and basil thrive together and repel common pests.
- Lettuce grows in tomato shade, preventing bolting.
- Pole beans fix nitrogen in the soil, feeding other plants.
- Carrots aerate the soil, creating better water drainage.

Yield Example: Fresh tomatoes, crisp lettuce, aromatic basil, crunchy carrots, and nutritious beans.

The Salad and Snack Garden (8x8 feet Raised Bed) Focus: Quick-growing crops for fresh harvests all season.

This layout is ideal for gardeners who want continuous harvests and variety in their meals.

Layout Plan:

- **Front Row (Closest to Sun)**
  - ❑ **Radishes (16 plants)** - Fast-growing root vegetables.
  - ❑ **Spinach (10 plants)** - Grows quickly in spring and fall.
- **Middle Row (Mix of Quick Harvest and Slow Growers)**
  - ❑ **Cherry Tomatoes (2 plants, staked)** - Small fruit, continuous harvest.
  - ❑ **Cucumbers (2 plants, trellis)** - Vertical growth maximizes space.
- **Back Row (North Side)**
  - ❑ **Snap Peas (6 plants, trellis)** - Easy to grow and productive.
  - ❑ **Lettuce (4 plants)** - Grows in the shade provided by taller plants.
- **Corners (For Pest Control and Pollinators)**
  - ❑ **Nasturtiums (4 plants)** - Edible flowers and natural pest repellents.

Key Benefits:

- Quick crops like radishes and spinach provide near-instant results.
- Vertical growth (cucumbers and snap peas) optimizes space.
- Nasturtiums add beauty and pest control.
- Continuous harvest from tomatoes, cucumbers, and lettuce keeps fresh produce on the table.

Yield Example: Crunchy radishes, leafy greens, cherry tomatoes, fresh cucumbers, and sweet snap peas-all perfect for summer salads and snacks.

As we conclude our exploration of designing your space for maximum yield, remember that each method we've discussed-from vertical gardens to rooftop beekeeping and container farming-offers unique ways to transform your environment. These techniques are not just about maximizing harvests; they're about creating spaces that reflect your values and aspirations. In the next chapter, we'll dive into growing your own food, taking the systems we've developed and exploring how they translate into a bountiful, sustainable harvest.

3

GROWING YOUR OWN FOOD: FROM SEED TO HARVEST

There's something truly miraculous about planting a tiny seed and watching it grow into something vibrant and alive. It's not magic-it's God's creation at work, a beautiful display of His design and care. Each seed is a testament to His provision, carrying the potential to nourish, sustain, and bring beauty into our lives. Heirloom seeds, in particular, tell a story of resilience and faithfulness passed down through generations. Every variety holds a legacy-a small miracle designed to thrive and adapt. When I first discovered heirloom seeds, I realized I wasn't just planting food; I was witnessing God's handiwork in action, a connection to His creation, and a way to honor His blessings. These seeds remind us not only of our responsibility to nurture the earth but also of the joy of trusting God's plan for growth and abundance.

Heirloom seeds are open-pollinated and non-hybrid, meaning they come from plants that have been pollinated naturally, often by wind, insects, or birds. This process ensures that the seeds are true to type, preserving the unique characteristics of each variety. Unlike hybrid seeds, which are bred for specific traits and do not reproduce true to type, heirlooms maintain genetic diversity. This diversity is crucial for resilience against diseases and pests, as it provides a gene bank of traits that might be lost in modern commercial varieties. Growing heirloom plants is like being part of a living museum, where each plant contributes to the historical tapestry of agriculture. By choosing heirloom seeds, you're playing a role in preserving these varieties for future generations, ensuring that their stories continue to be told.

The benefits of growing a variety of heirloom plants extend beyond mere aesthetics or flavor. Biodiversity is fundamental to a healthy and sustainable ecosystem. When you plant a diverse array of heirloom varieties, you enhance genetic diversity within your garden.

This diversity acts as an insurance policy against potential threats like plant diseases or changing climate conditions. By cultivating different species, you attract a wider range of beneficial insects. These insects, such as pollinators and natural predators, contribute to pest control, reducing the need for chemical interventions. A biodiverse garden is a resilient one, capable of withstanding challenges that might decimate a monoculture.

Moreover, the varied plant life supports a rich tapestry of soil microorganisms, further enhancing soil health and productivity.

When choosing the right heirloom seeds for your garden, consider your climate and gardening goals. Regional seed libraries and exchanges can be invaluable resources, offering varieties that are well-suited to your local conditions. These seeds have often been passed down by local gardeners who have selected them for their adaptability to regional climates. Seed catalogs specializing in heirlooms provide detailed descriptions, helping you select varieties that align with your taste preferences and gardening objectives. Whether you're looking for a tomato with exceptional flavor, a squash with a history of drought resistance, or a bean that attracts pollinators, there's an heirloom variety to meet your needs. By selecting seeds that are adapted to your environment, you increase the likelihood of a bountiful harvest.

Saving seeds from your heirloom plants is a rewarding practice that closes the loop on your gardening efforts. Start by choosing the healthiest, most vigorous plants from which to save seeds, as these will carry the traits you want to preserve. Allow the seeds to mature fully on the plant before harvesting them. Proper drying and storage are crucial to maintaining seed viability. Spread seeds out in a single layer in a cool, dry, and dark place until they are completely dry. Once dried, store them in airtight containers, such as glass jars or metal tins, labeled with the plant variety and date of collection. Keep these containers in a cool, dark location to extend their shelf life. Record-keeping is an often-overlooked step but is essential to track which seeds perform best in your garden. Detailed notes allow you to refine your choices each season, ensuring continuous improvement and adaptation.

Seed-Saving Checklist

- **Choose Healthy Plants:** Start with robust plants for seed saving.
- **Allow Full Maturity:** Let seeds mature on the plant before harvesting.
- **Dry Seeds Thoroughly:** Spread seeds to dry in a cool, dark place.
- **Store Seeds Properly:** Use airtight containers and label them.
- **Keep Records:** Note plant performance for future reference.

By engaging with heirloom seeds, you're doing more than cultivating a garden. You're participating in a legacy of agricultural history and biodiversity. Each seed holds within it the potential to enrich your garden and contribute to the wider ecosystem.

Climate-Specific Gardening Techniques

Gardening is deeply tied to the climate of your region and understanding this bond can transform your efforts. Tailoring your gardening practices to suit specific climatic conditions is not only practical but essential for success. Each garden has its own microclimates-those small areas where the conditions might differ slightly from the overall climate. A sunny corner shielded from the wind can become a perfect spot for heat loving plants, while a shaded area may nurture cool-season crops. Take time to observe these subtle variations in your garden. Track how the light shifts throughout the day, notice where the wind tends to blow strongest, and feel where the soil holds moisture longest.

These observations will guide your planting decisions, helping you choose the right plant for the right spot. Modifying your planting schedules based on regional weather patterns is also crucial. If you live in an area with late frosts, for example, you might start seeds indoors to give them a head start. Conversely, in warmer regions, you might delay planting until the intense heat subsides, ensuring that young plants aren't scorched by the sun.

Understanding your climate allows you to synchronize your gardening efforts with nature's cycles, optimizing growth and yield.

Water Management Techniques For A Resilient Garden

Water management becomes paramount as climates vary. In arid regions, conserving water is critical. Drip irrigation systems can be a game-changer, delivering water directly to the plant's roots, minimizing waste, and ensuring each plant gets exactly what it needs. These systems are not only efficient but also relatively easy to install. They can be customized to fit any garden size, from a few pots on a balcony to an expansive backyard.

Rainwater harvesting is another sustainable practice that benefits gardens across climates. Collecting rainwater in barrels during wet seasons provides a reservoir to draw from during drier times. This method not only reduces reliance on municipal water supplies but also helps manage runoff, preventing soil erosion and nutrient depletion.

On our homestead, we rely on a wobble head sprinkler system to water our 40x60-foot garden. This simple yet highly effective tool mimics rainfall, ensuring even water distribution across a large area. Paired with a pump that draws from our groundwater pond, it's a cost-effective solution that keeps our garden thriving without burdening municipal resources.

Mulching is another simple yet powerful method. By adding a thick layer of organic mulch such as straw, wood chips, or compost-around our plants, we reduce evaporation, regulate soil temperature, and suppress weeds that compete for water resources.

For your row crops and raised beds, soaker hoses offer targeted irrigation. These porous hoses deliver water directly to the soil along their length, minimizing evaporation and runoff.

In smaller garden beds, you can also experiment with ollas, unglazed clay pots buried near plants. Filled with water, they slowly release moisture directly to the roots through their porous walls, reducing both waste and evaporation.

For those with a bit of technical savvy, smart irrigation systems are worth exploring. These systems monitor soil moisture and weather forecasts, automatically adjusting watering schedules to prevent overwatering or underwatering.

In larger garden designs, swales and contour gardening are highly effective. Swales are shallow trenches dug along the natural contours of the land, capturing rainwater and allowing it to seep into the soil slowly. Paired with contour gardening, where crops are planted along the natural curves of the land, water retention is optimized.

We've also found that planting cover crops, such as clover or vetch, helps protect and enrich our soil. These living mulches retain moisture, prevent erosion, and add valuable nutrients to the earth.

Additionally, we've integrated windbreaks and shade structures into our homestead layout. Trees, shrubs, and shade cloths reduce evaporation caused by harsh winds and intense sun, creating microclimates where plants can thrive with less water stress.

Lastly, our raised garden beds are equipped with water reservoirs, allowing water to be stored and slowly released to plant roots, ensuring consistent hydration without constant attention.

By combining these water management techniques, you can create a resilient garden capable of thriving despite changing weather patterns. Each method serves a unique purpose, and together, they form a water-wise system tailored to your homestead's specific needs. Whether you're working with a large space or a small plot, intentional water management can maximize productivity while minimizing waste.

Soil Health: The Foundation Of A Thriving Garden

Soil is the foundation of any successful garden, and its fertility must be tailored to your local conditions. Healthy soil isn't just dirt-it's a living ecosystem full of microorganisms, organic matter, and essential nutrients. Understanding your soil's composition is the first step toward creating a thriving garden.

Testing Your Soil:

Before adding amendments, it's crucial to know what your soil needs. You can purchase an at-home soil testing kit or send a sample to your local agricultural extension office for professional analysis. A good soil test will measure key components like **pH levels, nitrogen (N), phosphorus (P),** and **potassium (K).** Ideal levels for most vegetable gardens are:

- **pH:** Between **6.0-7.0** (slightly acidic to neutral)
- **Nitrogen (N):** Vital for leafy green growth
- **Phosphorus (P):** Essential for root development and flowering
- **Potassium (K):** Important for overall plant health and disease resistance

If your soil is too acidic or too alkaline, amendments like lime or sulfur can help balance the pH. Regular testing-aim for at least once a year-will ensure your soil remains balanced and productive.

Composting is one of the best ways to improve soil fertility. It recycles kitchen scraps and yard waste into nutrient-rich humus, which acts as both a soil amendment and a natural fertilizer. To create effective compost:

- **Green materials (high nitrogen):** Grass clippings, vegetable scraps, coffee grounds
- **Brown materials (high carbon):** Dry leaves, straw, cardboard

The ideal compost pile should have a **2:1 ratio of brown to green materials** to maintain proper decomposition. Turn your compost regularly to aerate it and speed up the process. In cooler climates, high-nitrogen materials like grass clippings can help kickstart decomposition, while in warmer regions, carbon-rich brown materials like leaves help regulate the breakdown.

Animal manure is another excellent soil amendment, but it must be used carefully. **Cow manure,** for example, is rich in nutrients but needs to be aged or composted for **6-12 months** before being applied to the garden. Fresh manure can "burn" plants due to high ammonia levels and may carry pathogens. Well-composted manure not only boosts nitrogen and organic matter but also improves soil structure and moisture retention.

Cover crops like clover, vetch, or rye grass, are planted specifically to be tilled back into the soil. They help prevent erosion, suppress weeds, and add organic matter when decomposed. For best results, plant cover crops in the fall or early spring, allow them to grow until they flower, then cut them down and till them into the soil.

A thick layer of organic mulch, such as straw, wood chips, or shredded leaves, helps regulate soil moisture, reduce evaporation, suppress weeds, and add nutrients as it breaks down. Apply **2-4 inches of mulch** around plants, taking care not to pile it against stems, which can cause rot.

To maintain soil fertility, practice **crop rotation**-avoid planting the same crop in the same spot every year. This prevents soil depletion and minimizes pest and disease buildup.

Companion planting, where plants with complementary nutrient needs are grown together, can also optimize soil health.

Healthy soil is alive with microorganisms, earthworms, and fungi that play a crucial role in breaking down organic matter and making nutrients available to plants. Avoid synthetic chemicals and pesticides, as they can harm these beneficial organisms.

By understanding your soil's needs, incorporating organic amendments, and adopting sustainable practices like composting, mulching, and crop rotation, you create an environment where plants can thrive. Soil health is a long-term investment, and with time and care, it will reward you with abundant harvests season after season.

Extreme temperature variations pose significant challenges for gardeners, but with the right techniques, plants can be shielded from these stresses. Frost protection is vital for early and late-season gardening. Row covers made from lightweight fabric can provide a few degrees of warmth, protecting tender plants from unexpected cold snaps. These covers can be easily draped over plants and anchored with stones or soil, offering a simple yet effective solution. For those in areas with intense summer heat, shade cloths can prevent plants from wilting under the harsh sun. These cloths can be stretched over frames or trellises, offering respite to heat-sensitive crops. Cold frames, which are essentially minigreenhouses, extend the growing season by trapping solar energy and insulating plants.

They are particularly useful for hardening off seedlings in spring or growing hardy greens through the winter. Constructing a cold frame is a rewarding DIY project that requires only a few materials, such as old windows and lumber. This tool offers gardeners a greater degree of control over their growing environment, allowing for the cultivation of crops beyond the typical growing season.

By adapting your gardening techniques to your climate, you create a harmonious partnership with the land. This approach not only enhances the productivity of your garden but also deepens your connection to the natural rhythms of your environment. Each climate presents its own set of challenges and opportunities, and by embracing them, you empower your garden to thrive.

Troubleshooting Common Plant Pests

Gardening is a rewarding endeavor, but even a carefully tended garden can fall prey to pesky invaders. Recognizing the early signs of pest infestations is crucial to keeping your plants healthy and thriving. Have you ever noticed small holes in your kale leaves or wilting beans despite ample water? These are visual indicators that pests might be at play. Aphids, those tiny green or black insects, often cluster on the undersides of leaves, leaving behind a sticky residue known as honeydew. Slugs and snails, notorious for their nocturnal feasts, leave silvery trails and ragged holes in tender foliage. Then there are cabbage worms, small but mighty caterpillars that can decimate your brassicas overnight. Each pest leaves its own unique signature, a clue to its presence that you can learn to identify.

While conventional pesticides might seem like a quick fix, they can harm beneficial insects and disrupt the ecological balance of your garden. Instead, consider organic approaches that target pests without collateral damage. Introducing beneficial insects is a natural way to manage pest populations. Ladybugs, for instance, are voracious predators of aphids, while lacewings can tackle a variety of soft-bodied pests. You can purchase these helpful allies from garden centers or online suppliers, releasing them in the early evening when temperatures are cooler. Companion planting is another effective strategy. By interplanting flowers and herbs that repel specific pests, you create a defensive perimeter around your crops. Marigolds, with their pungent scent, deter nematodes, while basil can confuse and repel mosquitoes and flies. These plants not only protect but also add beauty and diversity to your garden.

Designing a pest-resistant garden involves more than just choosing the right plants; it's about fostering an environment that naturally discourages unwanted visitors. Diversifying plant species is a powerful tool. A mixed planting of vegetables, herbs, and flowers can confuse pests, making it harder for them to locate their preferred host plants. This approach also reduces the risk of a single pest wiping out your entire crop. Encouraging natural predators by providing habitats, such as rocks for lizards or small ponds for frogs, can further bolster your garden's defenses. These creatures will patrol your garden, keeping pest populations in check. Additionally, maintaining healthy soil through organic practices ensures that your plants are robust and better equipped to withstand pest pressure.

Regular monitoring and maintenance are your best defenses against pest problems. Set up pest monitoring traps, such as yellow sticky traps, to capture and identify flying insects.

These traps provide a snapshot of pest activity, allowing you to act before a minor issue becomes a major infestation. Routine inspections are equally important. Make it a habit to walk through your garden every day or at least every few days, looking closely at the undersides of leaves and the base of plants. Early detection allows for quick intervention, whether that's physically removing pests by hand or applying a targeted treatment like neem oil. Consistent care and attention will help you catch problems early, minimizing damage and keeping your garden vibrant and productive.

By embracing a holistic approach to pest management, you not only protect your crops but also contribute to a more sustainable and balanced ecosystem. Each step, from identifying pests to implementing organic controls, builds resilience in your garden, allowing it to flourish with life and vitality.

3.4 Maximizing Harvests in Limited Spaces

Growing your own food in a confined space can feel like a puzzle, but with a few thoughtful strategies, you can transform even the smallest plot into a prolific garden. One technique that stands out is efficient plant spacing, which ensures that every inch of your garden is put to good use. The square-foot gardening method is a fantastic way to organize your plants. By dividing your available space into square-foot sections, you can plan exactly where each plant will go. This approach not only maximizes your yield but also makes it easier to manage your garden. Each square foot becomes a mini garden, where you can plant specific crops based on their space requirements. For example, you might plant a single tomato plant in one square, while another square could hold a couple of radishes or a small bunch of herbs. This method encourages intensive planting, which helps to crowd out weeds and makes the most of limited space.

For example, in a **4x6-foot garden bed (24 square feet),** you can grow an impressive mix of produce while maintaining easy access for planting, watering, and harvesting.

Suggested Layout (Using 24 Squares) Vegetables (14 Squares)

1. **Tomatoes (1 square, 1 plant)** - Indeterminate variety; stake or cage for vertical growth.
2. **Cucumbers (1 square, 2 plants)** -Trellis to save space.
3. **Bell Peppers (1 square, 1 plant)** - Choose sweet bell peppers for versatility.
4. **Lettuce (2 squares, 4 plants per square)** - Leaf or romaine varieties; succession plant for extended harvest.
5. **Carrots (2 squares, 16 plants per square)** - Plant in loose, well-drained soil.
6. **Radishes (1 square, 16 plants)** - Quick harvest and a great companion to carrots.
7. **Green Beans (1 square, 4 plants)** - Use bush beans for compact growth.
8. **Zucchini (1 square, 1 plant)** - Grow compact or bush varieties.
9. **Spinach (2 squares, 9 plants per square)** - Cool-weather crop; can be succession planted.
10. **Kale (1 square, 1 plant)** - Nutritious and hardy leafy green.
11. **Onions (1 square, 9 plants)** - Plant green onions or small bulb varieties.

Herbs (6 Squares)

1. **Basil (1 square, 1 plant)** - Great companion to tomatoes.
2. **Parsley (1 square, 1 plant)** - Harvest frequently to encourage growth.
3. **Thyme (1 square, 1 plant)** - Low maintenance and fragrant.
4. **Chives (1 square, 4 plants)** - Adds flavor and repels pests.
5. **Cilantro (1 square, 1 plant)** - Best for cooler seasons.

6. **Oregano (1 square, 1 plant)** - Great for Mediterranean dishes.

Fruits (4 Squares)

1. **Strawberries (2 squares, 4 plants per square)** - Perennial and productive in compact spaces.
2. **Blueberries (2 squares, 1 bush per square)** - Requires acidic soil (consider growing in containers within the bed).

Garden Layout Plan Example

- **Row 1 (Back/Vertical Support):** Tomatoes (1), Cucumbers (1), Green Beans (1), Zucchini (1)
- **Row 2:** Bell Pepper (1), Kale (1), Spinach (2)
- **Row 3:** Carrots (2), Radishes (1), Lettuce (2)
- **Row 4:** Onions (1), Basil (1), Parsley (1), Cilantro (1)
- **Row 5:** Thyme (1), Chives (1), Oregano (1)
- **Row 6 (Front Row/Low-Growing Crops):** Strawberries (2), Blueberries (2)

This **4x6-foot garden plan** will provide a balanced mix of vegetables, fruits, and herbs, ensuring variety, productivity, and visual appeal while being manageable for beginners and seasoned gardeners alike.

Successive planting is another powerful strategy to ensure a continuous yield. By staggering plantings, you can harvest crops in waves, keeping your garden productive throughout the growing season. This means planning crop rotations carefully, so that as one crop finishes, another is ready to take its place. For instance, after harvesting early spring lettuce, you might plant beans in the same spot, followed by a fall crop of kale.

Timing is crucial here. Consider the days to maturity for each plant and work backward from your first expected frost date to ensure they have enough time to grow. By planning in cycles, you maintain a steady supply of fresh produce, avoiding the feast-or-famine cycle that can happen when everything ripens at once.

In small spaces, vertical and layered gardening can be your secret weapon. By growing up instead of out, you effectively double or triple your growing area. Implementing tiered planters is one way to achieve this. These structures allow you to stack plants, creating a lush, layered effect. You can also train vines like cucumbers or beans, to grow on trellises or arches. This not only saves space but also makes harvesting easier, as the fruits dangle at eye level. Vertical gardening also improves air circulation around plants, reducing the risk of disease. Consider using hanging baskets for trailing crops, or wall planters to turn a sunny wall into a living tapestry of greenery. These methods add dimension to your garden and make it possible to grow a wider variety of plants without needing more ground space.

Choosing high-yield varieties is essential for maximizing harvests in tight quarters. Look for dwarf or bush varieties that are specifically bred for compact gardens. These plants often produce as much fruit as their larger counterparts but take up significantly less room.

For instance, bush beans and patio tomatoes are perfect for containers and small plots, offering abundant harvests without sprawling out of control. Similarly, select crops known for their prolific production, like zucchini or small-fruited cherry tomatoes. These plants can provide a generous yield from a single plant, making them ideal choices for space conscious gardeners.

As you integrate these techniques into your gardening practice, remember that every space has its potential. Whether you're working with a small balcony, a narrow side yard, or a corner of your kitchen, these strategies can help you maximize your harvest and enjoy a bountiful supply of homegrown goodness. By using efficient spacing, successive planting, vertical gardening, and selecting the right varieties, you're not just growing food-you're cultivating a connection to your space and your resources. These methods empower you to take control of your food supply, even in the most limited settings, making your garden a testament to innovation and resilience.

In exploring these strategies, you lay the groundwork for a garden that thrives, regardless of size. Each plant becomes a part of a larger ecosystem, working together to create abundance. As we wrap up this chapter, consider how these practices can be applied to your unique space, nurturing both the land and your connection to it.

4

SUSTAINABLE LIVESTOCK PRACTICES FOR BEGINNERS

When we first added chickens to our homestead, the idea seemed both exciting and a little intimidating. A friend generously gifted us our first flock, and while we were living in town-not the countryside-we were eager to embrace this new adventure. Chickens are often the gateway livestock for many homesteaders, offering a taste of rural living right in your backyard. But the journey from curious novices to confident keepers was filled with questions. Which breeds are best for a small yard? How do we design a coop that fits our space and keeps the hens safe? These were just some of the questions swirling in our minds as we began this chapter. My hope is to guide you through these initial steps, sharing insights and practical tips that can ease your transition into keeping chickens, no matter where you live.

4.1 Chickens in Urban Settings

Selecting the right chicken breed is crucial for urban settings, where space is limited and neighbors are close. You'll want breeds that are not only hardy but also calm and quiet. Bantam breeds are a wonderful choice for small urban coops. These miniature chickens are only about half the size of standard breeds, requiring less space and food. Despite their size, they lay delightfully small, colorful eggs that are a joy to collect. Bantam Easter Eggers, for example, offer a rainbow of egg colors and are known for their friendly disposition. Their smaller stature makes them ideal for confined spaces, where every inch counts. Another excellent option is the Australorp, a quiet breed known for its prolific egg-laying and easygoing nature. With their glossy black feathers and gentle temperament, Australorps are a favorite among urban chicken keepers. Silkies, with their fluffy plumage and calm demeanor, are another breed that thrives in quieter environments. Their unique appearance and sweet nature make them a hit with families and children.

While chickens are a popular choice, urban homesteaders might also consider quail as an alternative. Quail require far less space than chickens, making them an appealing option for smaller yards or even balconies. These tiny birds are quiet, produce small but delicious eggs, and mature quickly, allowing for a faster yield of both eggs and meat. Quail coops are smaller and easier to maintain, and their waste can also be composted effectively. For those with extremely limited space or zoning restrictions on chickens, quail can be a practical and rewarding alternative.

Designing a chicken coop (or quail hutch) for an urban backyard requires some creativity and planning. You'll need to consider the coop's size, ensuring it accommodates your flock while fitting within your space constraints. For small chicken flocks, a coop of about 2-4 square feet per bird is generally sufficient. This ensures they have enough room to move comfortably without feeling crowded. When space is tight, consider vertical designs that incorporate perches and nesting boxes at different levels. Integrating predator-proof features is essential, even in urban areas. Raccoons, hawks, and even neighborhood cats can pose a threat. Secure latches, buried fencing, and sturdy construction can help keep your chickens or quail safe. Source 2 offers various DIY coop plans, from A-frame designs to mobile coops, providing flexibility to suit different urban landscapes.

Feeding and caring for chickens or quail in an urban environment can be streamlined with the right tools and routines. Space-saving feeders and waterers are great, allowing you to provide nourishment without cluttering the coop. Look for feeders that minimize waste and are easy to refill. Incorporating kitchen scraps into your chickens' diet is a fantastic way to reduce waste and offer them variety. Chickens love vegetable peels, stale bread, and leftover rice, turning your kitchen waste into nutritious meals. However, avoid giving them anything too salty or sugary, and steer clear of foods like onions and chocolate, which can be harmful.

Urban chicken keeping does come with its challenges, but these can be managed with thoughtful solutions. Noise control is a common concern, especially with neighbors nearby. Choosing quiet breeds helps, but additional measures like soundproofing can make a difference. You might line the coop with insulation or position it away from shared fences to buffer sound.

Waste management is another consideration. Chicken manure is a valuable resource when composted properly, enriching your garden and reducing disposal needs. One highly effective method is deep litter composting using pine shavings. This technique involves layering fresh pine shavings over chicken droppings regularly, allowing them to break down over time into a rich, compost-like material. This not only helps control odors but also reduces the frequency of cleaning and provides an excellent soil amendment for your garden.

Whether you choose chickens, quail, or a combination of both, urban poultry keeping offers a rewarding path toward self-sufficiency. Your small backyard can become a thriving hub of productivity and connection to nature with proper planning, the right breeds, and sustainable waste management practices.

Building a Vertical Chicken Coop for Small Backyards

A vertical chicken coop is an excellent solution for limited backyard space. Its compact, multi-level design provides adequate room for your chickens while maximizing vertical space for perches, nesting boxes, and ventilation. Below is a simple list of materials needed and step-by-step instructions for how to build something for your homestead. Remember, you can make your chicken coop any way you wish. This is just a starting point to get you going. You can find hundreds of other coop plans online.

Materials Needed:

- **Lumber:** 2x4s and plywood sheets
- **Nesting Boxes:** Pre-made or custom wooden boxes (1 per 3-4 chickens)
- **Wire Mesh:** Predator-proof, galvanized hardware cloth
- **Roofing Material:** Metal or corrugated plastic
- **Hinges and Latches:** Secure, weatherproof hardware
- **Ventilation Panels:** Wire mesh-covered openings near the roofline
- **Screws and Nails:** Weather-resistant

Step 1: Build the Frame

- Start by constructing a rectangular base frame (approx. 4x4 ft).
- Build vertical corner posts (at least 4 ft high) to create a multi-level structure.
- Attach horizontal supports to form two levels: a lower area for shelter and an upper area for nesting boxes and perches.

Step 2: Add Nesting Boxes

- Attach nesting boxes at an accessible height on the upper level (approx. 1 ft above the ground).
- Ensure they have a hinged lid for easy egg collection.

Step 3: Install Perches

- Add wooden dowels or sturdy branches at varying heights inside the coop.
- Ensure there's enough space for each chicken to roost comfortably.

Step 4: Secure with Wire Mesh

- Cover the lower section and windows with predator-proof wire mesh.
- Bury the mesh 6 inches into the ground around the perimeter to prevent predators from digging underneath.

Step 5: Add Doors and Latches

- Install a large access door for cleaning and maintenance.
- Use sturdy latches to keep the door secure against raccoons and other predators.

Step 6: Ventilation and Roofing

- Add ventilation panels near the roofline to ensure proper airflow.
- Install a slanted roof to allow rain and snow to slide off easily.

Step 7: Create a Run (Optional)

- Attach a small fenced-in chicken run connected to the coop to allow outdoor roaming.

Maintenance Tips:

- Clean nesting boxes weekly and replace bedding regularly.
- Check latches and wire mesh frequently for damage.
- Ensure ventilation openings remain unobstructed.

With this guidance, urban chicken keeping can become a rewarding aspect of your homesteading lifestyle, offering fresh eggs and the joy of feathered companions.

4.2 Beekeeping: A Journey of Trial, Error, and Discovery

Beekeeping is often described as opening a window into one of nature's most fascinating and intricate systems. Bees are tiny powerhouses of productivity and cooperation, and observing their world is both humbling and inspiring. On our homestead, we've had our fair share of beekeeping adventures and misadventures. We've tried and failed at beekeeping twice using the conventional Langstroth method. The first time, our hive was overrun by ants, and the second, a neighbor sprayed their fields with chemicals and devastated our colony. Those experiences were heartbreaking, but they also taught us valuable lessons and pushed us to explore a more natural approach to beekeeping-one that works in harmony with the bees' natural instincts.

At its core, beekeeping is about understanding and respecting the bees. A hive is a finely tuned society with a clear structure and purpose. The **queen bee** is the heart of the hive, laying up to 2,000 eggs a day during peak seasons. Her pheromones maintain harmony and order. The **worker bees,** all female, are the lifeblood of the colony. They progress through different roles in their short lives: nurse bees caring for larvae, guards protecting the hive, and foragers collecting nectar and pollen. The **drones,** the male bees, have one simple task-to mate with a queen. Though their role might seem limited, it's essential for the colony's survival.

The Industrial (Conventional) Approach: Langstroth Hives

The **Langstroth hive** is one of the most common hive designs, favored for its modular, stackable structure. It consists of vertically stacked boxes with removable frames, allowing beekeepers to inspect the hive easily and harvest honey with minimal disruption. It's a system that works well in commercial setups, but it also has its drawbacks. Every time you inspect the hive, you must lift heavy boxes (40-100 pounds) and disrupt the colony's natural order. The queen's pheromones can become scattered, and the bees can become agitated, associating the beekeeper with trauma. Additionally, the thin wooden walls of Langstroth hives don't provide optimal insulation in extreme weather conditions.

While Langstroth hives are productive and efficient, they may not always align with the goals of a homesteader seeking a more natural and low-intervention approach to beekeeping.

However, if managed with care, they can still offer a productive and fulfilling beekeeping experience.

The Natural Approach: Horizontal Hives and Native Swarms

After our initial struggles, we discovered the **horizontal hive,** specifically the **Layens hive.** These hives mimic the natural cavities bees would select in the wild, such as hollowed-out trees. The thick wooden walls provide superior insulation, keeping bees warm in winter and cool in summer. Unlike vertical Langstroth hives, inspections in a Layens hive are far less invasive. You can lift one frame at a time without disturbing the entire colony.

One significant advantage of the Layens hive is its **frame design.** The frames are tall rather than wide, mimicking how bees naturally build their honeycomb. The honey is stored in a distinctive "honey rainbow" pattern at the top of the frames, providing an uninterrupted food source during winter. With fewer disturbances and better insulation, bees are calmer and less prone to aggressive behavior.

Catching a Native Swarm

One of the most exciting aspects of natural beekeeping is catching a **wild swarm** and relocating it to your homestead. Swarming is how bees naturally reproduce and expand their colonies. In the spring and summer, when resources are abundant, a colony will prepare a new queen, and the old queen will leave the hive with a group of worker bees to establish a new home.

To attract a swarm, you'll need a **swarm trap.** These are small hive boxes baited with lemongrass essential oil, which mimics the scent of a queen bee. Once a swarm moves into the trap, it must be carefully relocated to your permanent hive. This process requires patience, a steady hand, and a well-prepared smoker to keep the bees calm during the transition.

When transferring a swarm into a Layens or Langstroth hive, it's crucial to keep the frames in the same order as they were in the trap. These frames will become the colony's **brood nest,** where the queen lays her eggs. The success of your colony often hinges on this delicate transfer, so approach it with care and attention.

Bee Behavior and Hive Maintenance

Whether you're using a Langstroth or Layens hive, understanding bee behavior is essential. Bees are highly organized, with each part of the hive serving a distinct purpose:

- **Resource Frames:** These outermost frames store honey and bee bread (a protein rich mixture of pollen and nectar).
- **Brood Nest:** The center of the hive where eggs are laid and larvae grow.
- **Worker Bees:** Perform vital tasks such as cleaning, feeding larvae, guarding, and foraging.
- **Drones:** Males that mate with virgin queens during swarm season.

Hive Inspections

Routine inspections are necessary but should be done thoughtfully. Use a **smoker** with cool smoke to calm the bees. Open the hive from behind to minimize disturbance. Look for:

- Evidence of a **healthy queen** (eggs in the brood nest).
- Signs of pests like **Varroa mites or hive beetles.**
- Adequate honey reserves for the winter months.

Feeding and Supporting Your Bees

Bees are most productive when they can rely on natural nectar sources. Planting **bee friendly flowers** that bloom in spring, summer, and fall provides consistent resources. Avoid using sugar water unless absolutely necessary-it lacks the nutrients bees get from nectar and honey.

During summer **dearth periods** (when flowers stop blooming), bees rely on their stored honey. It's essential to leave enough honey for the colony to survive the winter. Always prioritize the bees' health over honey extraction.

Overcoming the Fear of Beekeeping

Fear is a common obstacle for new beekeepers. Bees can sense agitation and stress, and calm, confident handling goes a long way. Bee stings are rare if you handle your bees gently, wear proper protective clothing, and use a smoker correctly.

Remember: **Bees are not out to get you.** Their mission is to gather nectar, build their colony, and survive the winter. They are essential pollinators, responsible for one-third of the food we eat.

Final Thoughts on Beekeeping

Beekeeping isn't just about honey-it's about supporting a delicate ecosystem. Whether you choose a Langstroth hive for its modular efficiency or a Layens hive for its natural design, the key is to work *with* the bees, not against them. Pay attention to their needs, give them space to thrive, and approach your hive with care and respect.

On our homestead, beekeeping has become more than just another project. It's a way to connect with nature, foster resilience, and contribute to the health of our land. Whether you're harvesting honey, observing their mesmerizing flight patterns, or simply enjoying the hum of a healthy hive, beekeeping is a journey worth taking. With patience, care, and a little courage, you can build a thriving apiary and experience the profound joy of stewarding these incredible creatures.

4.3 Integrating Goats and Larger Livestock into Your Homestead

Bringing livestock onto your homestead is one of the most rewarding steps toward selfsufficiency. Whether it's goats, cows, sheep, or alpacas, each animal brings unique benefits and challenges. Over the years, we've learned a lot about raising these animals. Sometimes we learned the hard way, but every lesson has helped us grow closer to our goals.

We started our journey with **Miniature Nigerian Dwarf goats.** Their small size and sweet personalities made them a great choice for beginners. They required less space, were easier to handle, and gave us a small but steady supply of rich, creamy milk-perfect for yogurt and cheese-making. But as our family grew and our needs changed, we realized we wanted a larger milk supply. That's when we transitioned to **Nubian goats.** Their high milk production was impressive, and they gave us plenty of milk for both drinking and crafting homemade dairy products.

However, it wasn't until we tasted fresh **Jersey cow milk** from a neighbor that we realized what we'd been missing. The cream line, the taste, and the ease of making butter-it was everything we wanted. So, we took the leap and brought a **Jersey family cow** to our homestead. It wasn't an easy transition. Training a cow to be milked consistently and calmly required weeks of patience, gentle handling, and daily consistency. But the effort paid off, and today, our sweet Jersey cow is a beloved member of our farm and a reliable provider of delicious, nutrient-rich milk.

One of the most common concerns people have about owning a family milk cow is the **commitment to daily milking.** But here's the truth: you *don't have to milk every single day!* On our homestead, we always keep a **bull to breed our cow** and ensure she has a calf by her side. This means that if we want to take a break, travel, or simply skip a day of milking, the calf can nurse, and we don't have to worry about the cow's udder becoming engorged. It's an incredibly freeing system that still allows us to enjoy the benefits of fresh milk without feeling tied to the milking stand every single day. This approach has given us so much flexibility and balance in our homesteading life.

Choosing the Right Livestock for Your Needs

If you're trying to decide between goats and cows, start with your homestead goals:

- **Goats:** Great for small spaces, adaptable, and excellent for milk, meat, or fiber (depending on the breed). They are natural browsers and can thrive in areas where cows might struggle.
- **Cows:** Ideal for larger families or homesteads with more land. Jersey cows are known for their high butterfat milk, perfect for butter and cream. Meat breeds like Angus or Hereford are excellent choices for sustainable beef production.

For those interested in fiber production, **Angora goats** provide luxurious mohair, while sheep and alpacas produce wool and alpaca fleece, highly valued by crafters.

Fencing and Housing: Building Safe Spaces for Livestock

When it comes to fencing, goats are notorious escape artists. Our first goat fence was tested (and defeated) multiple times before we figured out the right setup. A **sturdy woven-wire fence,** reinforced with electric fencing, is essential. Regular inspections for gaps and weak points are necessary, as goats will always find that one loose spot to squeeze through.

Housing doesn't need to be complicated. For goats, a **simple three-sided shelter** works well in moderate climates, offering protection from wind and rain. In colder regions, an enclosed barn with good ventilation is better.

Cows, on the other hand, need a bit more space and sturdier structures. A **well-ventilated barn** or large shelter keeps them warm in winter and shaded in summer. Comfortable bedding, such as **straw or wood shavings,** ensures your animals are warm, dry, and happy year-round.

Feeding and Nutrition: Healthy Animals, Healthy Homestead

Nutrition is the foundation of healthy livestock.

- **Goats:** Thrive on a mix of high-quality hay, pasture, and supplemental goat feed rich in calcium and phosphorus. Goats are natural browsers, so letting them nibble on shrubs and plants enhances their health. Loose minerals and fresh water should always be available.
- **Cows:** Rely on high-quality pasture and hay, supplemented with grains or concentrates if they're producing milk. Jersey cows, in particular, need consistent access to quality forage and mineral supplements to maintain their health and milk production.

One thing we learned early on was the importance of body condition monitoring. Regularly checking your animals for signs of weight loss, illness, or deficiencies helps you adjust their feed and care before problems arise.

Training and Handling: Building Trust with Your Animals

Raising goats and cows isn't just about feeding and sheltering them-it's about building trust. Training a dairy animal, whether goat or cow, takes time, patience, and consistency.

With our goats, we made it a habit to handle them daily, even when they were still young. We touched their udders, guided them into the milking stand, and rewarded them with treats. This consistent handling made them much calmer and more cooperative when it came time for actual milking.

Our Jersey cow required even more patience. Cows are large animals, and gaining their trust takes daily effort. We spent weeks training her to the milking stand, ensuring she felt safe and comfortable. Over time, she learned to stand calmly and even seemed to enjoy our daily routine. As soon as she hears my voice she comes running.

Routine Care and Health Maintenance

Healthy animals require regular care and observation. For goats, **hoof trimming** is a must to prevent overgrowth and lameness. Routine health checks, including **deworming** and **vaccinations,** are equally important.

For cows, **hooves** should also be checked and trimmed as needed, but they typically don't grow as fast as goat hooves. Observing your animals daily is one of the best tools you have. Changes in appetite, behavior, or physical appearance are often the first signs of illness.

Building a relationship with a trusted **veterinarian** is invaluable. While many health concerns can be managed with basic knowledge, having an expert you can call when things get serious brings peace of mind.

The Reward of Livestock on a Homestead

Goats and cows have become an integral part of our homestead, not just for the milk and food they provide, but for the rhythm and routine they add to our lives. Milking when we want, preparing fresh butter, or simply watching them graze in the fields-these moments remind us why we chose this life in the first place.

If you're considering adding livestock to your homestead, start small, be patient, and don't be afraid to make mistakes. Every animal will teach you something new, and every season will bring opportunities to grow. Whether it's a sweet miniature goat or a gentle Jersey cow, the bond you build with your animals is one of the most rewarding parts of homesteading.

And trust me, there's nothing quite like fresh milk straight from your own backyard.

Make a Difference with Your Review
Unlock the Power of Sharing

"The smallest act of kindness is worth
more than the grandest intention."
- Oscar Wilde

When we set out to write *A Modern Guide to Homesteading,* our goal was simple: to share what we've learned, inspire others, and build a community of like-minded people who believe in sustainable, intentional living.

But reaching others-those who are just beginning their homesteading journey or those seeking new inspiration-depends on readers like *you.*

Most people choose books based on reviews. Your words have the power to guide someone, encourage them to take the leap, and show them that homesteading isn't just a dream-it's a reachable goal.

Your review might:

- Help one more family start their first garden.
- Encourage one more person to raise chickens or try beekeeping.
- Give one more homesteader the confidence to start small and dream big.
- Support one more household in embracing a more self-sufficient lifestyle.

It costs nothing and takes just a minute, but your review could spark a lifelong passion in someone else.

To leave a review and make a difference, simply scan the QR code below or visit:

From our homestead to yours, thank you from the bottom of our hearts for being a part of this journey.

Warmly,
Homestead Mentors

4.4 Ethical Practices in Animal Husbandry

When we raise animals, we're entrusted with their care and well-being, a responsibility that calls for a deep respect for their lives and needs. Ethical animal husbandry begins with providing adequate space and enrichment for your livestock. It's about more than just physical space; it's about creating an environment where animals can express their natural behaviors. This might mean ensuring goats have plenty of room to roam and climb, offering them obstacles and varied terrain that mimic their natural habitats. For cows, it could mean access to pastureland where they can graze freely and experience the changing seasons.

Enrichment is essential for mental stimulation. Simple additions like logs for goats to climb or toys for pigs can keep animals engaged and content. Humane treatment and handling are at the core of ethical care. This involves gentle interactions, understanding the body language and needs of your animals, and ensuring that they are handled calmly and confidently. It's about building a rapport based on trust and respect, which in turn makes managing them easier and more rewarding.

Sustainable feeding practices are another cornerstone of ethical animal husbandry. Choosing local and organic feed sources not only supports the health of your animals but also reduces your environmental impact. Local feeds minimize the carbon footprint associated with transportation, while organic options avoid the use of harmful chemicals and pesticides. These choices contribute to a healthier planet and healthier animals.

Efficient management of feed can also significantly reduce waste. This might involve using feeders that minimize spillage or training animals to eat at specific times to prevent overconsumption. Additionally, incorporating a variety of forages can enhance nutrition and stimulate natural feeding behaviors. Allowing livestock to graze on different plants not only diversifies their diet but also improves soil health and biodiversity on your homestead.

Managing livestock waste responsibly is crucial for both environmental health and the well-being of your animals. Composting manure is a sustainable solution that transforms waste into a valuable resource for your garden. This process not only reduces the volume of waste you produce but also enriches your soil with nutrients, promoting vigorous plant growth.

Ensure that compost piles are correctly managed, with the proper balance of carbon and nitrogen materials to accelerate decomposition and minimize odors. Waste can also be integrated into permaculture systems, where it supports a closed-loop cycle of nutrients. For instance, manure can be used in creating rich mulch or added to worm farms, where it's broken down into worm castings-an excellent organic fertilizer. These practices embody the principles of zero-waste living, turning potential pollutants into assets that support a thriving homestead ecosystem.

Fostering a symbiotic relationship with your livestock involves seeing them as partners in your homesteading efforts. This relationship is built on consistent care and understanding of animal behavior. Spend time observing your animals, learning their habits, and recognizing their individual personalities. This knowledge allows you to anticipate their needs and address any issues before they become problems. Building trust takes time but pays off in a smoother, more harmonious management routine. Engaging with your animals daily helps them become accustomed to your presence and build confidence in your handling. As you deepen this connection, you'll find that each animal contributes uniquely to your homestead, whether it's through milk, fiber, companionship, or simply the joy of their presence.

As we wrap up this chapter, consider how these practices can be integrated into your homesteading efforts. Whether you're caring for a small flock of chickens or managing a mixed herd of livestock, these principles offer a framework for ethical, sustainable animal care. In the next chapter, we'll explore the art of food preservation, turning the bounty of your homestead into delicious, lasting provisions that carry you through the seasons.

5

MASTERING THE ART OF FOOD PRESERVATION

Imagine standing in your kitchen, surrounded by jars of colorful vegetables, each one a testament to the bounty you've grown. The air is filled with the tangy aroma of fermenting cabbage, reminiscent of your first dive into fermentation. Food preservation is not just a skill; it's a bridge to the past, a way to savor the flavors of summer long after the seasons have changed. It connects us to traditions that have nourished families for generations. I remember my first attempt at creating sauerkraut. It was a simple mix of cabbage and salt, yet as it transformed, I found a connection to something ancient and deeply satisfying.

Fermentation is a fascinating dance with nature, a process that invites beneficial bacteria to break down sugars and transform foods into something delicious and nutritious.

Understanding the biochemical process of fermentation is like unlocking a secret code to preserve food naturally. At its core, fermentation relies on the work of beneficial bacteria and yeasts. These microorganisms convert the sugars present in food into acids, gases, or alcohol, depending on the type of fermentation.

Lacto-fermentation, for instance, involves bacteria called Lactobacillus, which convert sugars into lactic acid. This acid acts as a natural preservative, not only extending the shelf life of food but also enhancing its flavor and nutritional value. Unlike canning, which relies on heat to preserve food, fermentation is a living process where the food continues to evolve over time, developing depth and complexity. The tangy bite of sauerkraut or the spicy kick of kimchi owes its character to this remarkable transformation.

Fermentation brings a host of health benefits, primarily through its positive impact on gut health. The probiotics generated during fermentation help maintain a healthy balance of gut bacteria, supporting digestion and bolstering immunity. Incorporating fermented foods into your diet can improve nutrient absorption, making the vitamins and minerals in your food more bioavailable. This means your body can more efficiently use the nutrients you consume, enhancing overall health. Fermented vegetables like sauerkraut and kimchi are particularly beneficial, as they combine the fiber and nutrients of vegetables with the probiotic benefits of fermentation. These foods can help regulate digestion, reduce inflammation, and support the immune system, contributing to a balanced diet and wellbeing.

Starting with simple fermentation recipes is a wonderful way to dip your toes into this ancient practice. Making sauerkraut, for example, is as straightforward as shredding cabbage, massaging it with salt, and packing it tightly into a jar. The salt draws out the cabbage's natural juices, creating a brine that promotes the growth of beneficial bacteria while inhibiting harmful ones. Over the course of a few weeks, the cabbage transforms into tangy sauerkraut, rich in flavor and probiotics.

Kimchi, another beloved fermented food, combines napa cabbage with a spicy paste made from chili pepper, garlic, ginger, and fish sauce. The result is a vibrant, spicy condiment that can elevate any meal. Both of these recipes are forgiving and flexible, allowing you to adjust ingredients to your taste preferences.

Safety is paramount in fermentation, as maintaining the right conditions is essential for good results. The key to safe fermentation is creating and maintaining anaerobic conditions, meaning an environment devoid of oxygen. This is achieved by ensuring the food is submerged in brine, preventing exposure to air. Weights or fermentation lids can help keep vegetables submerged, reducing the risk of spoilage. It's important to recognize the signs of spoilage, such as unpleasant odors, mold growth, or unusual colors, which indicate that something has gone awry. Trust your senses; if something smells or looks off, it's best to discard it. Fermentation is generally safe when proper techniques are followed, but vigilance ensures your creations are both delicious and safe to eat.

Interactive Element: Fermentation Journal

Keep a fermentation journal to track your progress and observations. Note the following:

- **Recipe Used:** Ingredients and proportions.
- **Fermentation Time:** Duration and conditions.
- **Observations:** Changes in taste, smell, and texture.
- **Future Adjustments:** Improvements for next time.

This journal not only enhances your fermentation skills but also creates a personal record of your culinary journey, capturing the nuances of your experiments and the unique flavors you develop.

5.2 Canning Essentials for Beginners

Canning is one of those homesteading skills that feels like a rite of passage. It's a way to capture the fleeting essence of each season, transforming fresh, ripe produce into jars of preserved goodness that can be enjoyed all year long. Understanding the basic methods of canning is crucial, especially when you're just starting out. Water bath canning and pressure canning are the two primary techniques, with each being suited to different types of foods. Water bath canning is perfect for high-acid foods like fruits, jams, jellies, and pickles. The acidity in these foods, combined with the heat of boiling water, is sufficient to prevent spoilage. Pressure canning, on the other hand, is necessary for low-acid foods like vegetables, meats, and soups. These foods require higher temperatures to safely eliminate the risk of botulism, a rare but serious form of food poisoning.

Before you begin canning, gather the essential equipment for each method. For water bath canning, you'll need a large pot with a lid, a canning rack to keep jars off the bottom, and mason jars with two-piece lids. A jar lifter, funnel, and bubble remover are helpful tools to have on hand, as well.

Pressure canning requires a specialized pressure canner, which is different from a pressure cooker. This canner must have a pressure gauge or weight to regulate the pressure within. It's essential to follow the manufacturer's instructions to operate a pressure canner safely. With the right equipment, you're well on your way to preserving a pantry full of delicious, homemade foods.

The canning process itself is straightforward but requires attention to detail. Start by sterilizing your jars and lids to prevent contamination. This can be done by washing them in hot, soapy water and then boiling them for a few minutes. Once your jars are clean, fill them with your prepared food, leaving the recommended headspace to allow for expansion during processing. Use a bubble remover to release any trapped air, which can affect the seal. Wipe the jar rims clean, place the lids on top, and secure them with rings. For water bath canning, immerse the jars in boiling water, ensuring they are covered by at least an inch of water. Processing times vary based on the food type and altitude, so consult a reliable canning guide for specifics. Pressure canning follows a similar preparation process, but the jars are placed in the pressure canner, which is then sealed and brought to the required pressure for a specified time.

Top 5 Water Bath Canning Foods

Water bath canning is best for **high-acid foods** with a pH of **4.6 or lower,** like fruits, jams, and pickles.

Food	Processing Time	Jar Size	Altitude Adjustment	Notes
Tomato Sauce (with added acidity)	35-45 min	Pints/Quarts	Add 5 min over 1,000 ft	Add lemon juice or citric acid
Strawberry Jam	10 min	Half-pints	Add 5 min over 1,000 ft	Use ripe, high-auality fruit
Dill Pickles	10-15 min	Pints/Quarts	Add 5 min over 1,000 ft	Use pickling cucumbers
Peach Slices	25 min	Pints	Add 5 min over 1,000 ft	Use ripe, firm peaches
Apple Butter	10 min	Half- pints/ Pints	Add 5 min over 1,000 ft	Smooth consistency works best

General Tip: Always ensure at least **1 inch of water covers the jars** during the boiling process.

Top 5 Pressure Canning Foods

Pressure canning is essential for **low-acid foods** with a pH **above 4.6,** such as vegetables, meats, and soups.

Food	Processing Time	Pressure (PSI)	Jar Size	Altitude Adjustment	Notes
Green Beans	20-25 min	10 PSI	Pints	Increase PSI above 1,000 ft	Fresh, firm beans are best
Chicken (boneless)	75 min	10 PSI	Pints	Increase PSI above 1,000 ft	Raw or cooked meat works
Carrots	25-30 min	10 PSI	Pints	Increase PSI above 1,000 ft	Peel and slice evenly

Beef Stew	90 min	10 PSI	Quarts	Increase PSI above 1,000 ft	Pre-cook stew for safety
Potatoes	35 min	10 PSI	Quarts	Increase PSI above 1,000 ft	Use firm, waxy potatoes

General Tip: Always follow your pressure canner's manual for PSI adjustments based on **altitude** and **jar size.**

The importance of safety in canning cannot be overstated. Following proper guidelines is essential to prevent food borne illnesses. One of the most critical risks to be aware of is botulism, which can occur in improperly processed low-acid foods. Always use tested recipes and adhere strictly to processing times and temperatures. After processing, let the jars cool naturally, which allows the vacuum seal to form. Test seals by pressing the center of each lid. If it doesn't flex, the seal is good. If it pops up and down, the jar did not seal properly and should be refrigerated and used soon. Store sealed jars in a cool, dark place to maintain quality. Label them with the contents and date so you can enjoy them at their peak.

Canning opens up a world of creative possibilities in the kitchen, allowing you to savor the flavors of summer long after the season has passed. Two timeless favorites in home canning are **tomato sauce** and **strawberry jam,** both of which are simple, rewarding, and bursting with flavor.

Homemade Tomato Sauce Recipe

Capture the vibrant essence of summer tomatoes in every jar.

Ingredients:

- 5 lbs fresh tomatoes
- 4 cloves garlic, minced
- 1/4 cup fresh basil, chopped
- 2 tbsp olive oil
- 2 tbsp vinegar (white or apple cider)
- 1 tsp salt

Instructions:

1. **Blanch the Tomatoes:** Boil a pot of water and drop the tomatoes in for 1 minute. Remove and place them in ice water. Peel off the skins.
2. **Cook the Sauce:** In a large pot, heat olive oil and saute garlic. Add tomatoes, basil, vinegar, and salt. Simmer for 30-45 minutes.
3. **Blend and Jar:** Use an immersion blender to reach your desired consistency. Fill sterilized jars, leaving 1/2 inch of headspace.
4. **Process:** Water bath can for 35-45 minutes (adjust for altitude if needed).

This sauce is perfect for pasta, pizza, or any dish that calls for rich tomato goodness.

Simple Strawberry Jam Recipe

Enjoy the sweet taste of summer strawberries on your toast, desserts, or straight from the spoon!

Ingredients:

- 2 lbs fresh strawberries, hulled and mashed
- 4 cups granulated sugar
- 1/ 4 cup lemon juice
- 1 packet (1.75 oz) powdered fruit pectin

Instructions:

1. **Cook the Jam:** In a large pot, combine mashed strawberries, sugar, lemon juice, and pectin. Stir constantly over medium heat until it reaches a rolling boil.
2. **Skim Foam:** Remove any foam that forms on the top.
3. **Fill Jars:** Pour the hot jam into sterilized jars, leaving 1/4 inch of headspace.

4. **Process:** Water bath can for 10 minutes (adjust for altitude if needed).

This jam brings a burst of sweetness to breakfasts, baked goods, or even a scoop of vanilla ice cream.

Both of these recipes preserve the taste of fresh produce and offer a sense of accomplishment and joy. There's something truly special about opening a jar of homemade sauce or jam in the middle of winter-it's like tasting summer all over again. Happy canning!

5.3 Drying Techniques for Long-Term Storage

Food drying holds a special place in the realm of preservation, offering a practical way to extend the life of your harvest while maintaining the flavors and nutrients that make homegrown produce so rewarding. Unlike other methods, drying reduces the weight and bulk of foods, making them easy to store and transport. This lightweight, non-perishable form makes dried foods an excellent choice for those looking to stock up without taking up too much space. Drying also concentrates the natural sugars and flavors in fruits, creating treats that are both delicious and nutritious. Imagine biting into a sun-dried tomato and relishing its intense, sweet tang. This is a taste that can brighten any winter meal. The ability to preserve food by drying not only reduces waste but also ensures that nothing goes to waste, even when you have a bumper crop.

Best Foods for Drying

Not all foods are suited to drying, and choosing the right produce can make the difference between success and frustration. Here's a quick guide:

- **Fruits:** Apples, peaches, bananas, strawberries, tomatoes, mangoes

- **Vegetables:** Peppers, kale, carrots, mushrooms, zucchini, green beans
- **Herbs:** Basil, oregano, thyme, parsley, mint, rosemary
- **Meats:** Beef, turkey, venison (for jerky)

These foods are beginner-friendly and yield reliable results when dried correctly.

Traditional vs. Modern Drying Methods

Traditional drying methods, like sun-drying, have been used for centuries and remain popular for their simplicity and effectiveness. Picture a warm, sunny day with trays of sliced fruits and herbs spread out to bask under the sun's rays. This method works well in dry climates, where low humidity and consistent heat can efficiently remove moisture from foods. Sun-drying can be a communal activity, involving friends or family in the task of preparing and laying out the produce.

Modern food dehydrators offer an excellent alternative for those living in less predictable climates. These devices provide controlled temperatures and airflow, ensuring consistent results regardless of the weather outside. With a dehydrator, you can dry a wide variety of foods, from apple slices to kale chips, all while maintaining the nutritional integrity and flavor of the fresh produce. The convenience of a dehydrator allows for year-round drying, so you can preserve your seasonal bounty even in the depths of winter.

Preparing Foods for Drying

Preparing foods for drying is a crucial step to ensure even dehydration and optimal quality. Fruits often benefit from pre-treatment to prevent oxidation and maintain their vibrant colors. A quick dip in a solution of **lemon juice and water (1 tablespoon of lemon juice per cup of water)** can work wonders, preserving the natural hue of apples or peaches and preventing the unsightly browning that can occur during drying.

Slicing Tips: Use a mandolin or sharp knife to create uniform slices, about ¼ inch thick. Consistent slices ensure even drying and prevent some pieces from over-drying while others remain moist.

Simple Recipe: Apple Chips

- **Ingredients:** Fresh apples, lemon water, cinnamon (optional)
- **Steps:**
  1. Slice apples thinly and dip them in lemon water.
  2. Arrange slices on a dehydrator tray or baking sheet.
  3. Sprinkle lightly with cinnamon, if desired.
  4. Dry at **135°F for 6-8 hours** until crispy.
- **Storage Tip:** Once cooled, store apple chips in an airtight container.

Climate and Altitude Considerations

Humidity and altitude play a big role in drying efficiency:

- **High Humidity:** Foods may require longer drying times or a dehydrator for best results.
- **High Altitude:** Slight adjustments to drying temperature may be necessary since water boils at a lower temperature at higher altitudes.

A simple hygrometer can help monitor the humidity in your drying space for optimal results.

Creative Uses for Dried Foods

Dried foods aren't just for snacking! Here are a few ideas:

- **Sun-Dried Tomatoes:** Add to pasta or homemade pizza.
- **Dried Herbs:** Create your own seasoning blends.

- **Dried Fruit:** Perfect for trail mix, granola, or baking.
- **Vegetable Powders:** Blend dried vegetables into powders for soups or sauces.

Dried foods are pantry staples that can elevate everyday meals while reducing waste.

Troubleshooting Common Drying Problems

Even experienced homesteaders encounter drying issues. Here are solutions to common problems:

- **Food Browning During Drying:** Use lemon juice pre-treatment.
- **Mold on Dried Food:** Ensure food is completely dry before storing, and store in airtight containers.
- **Leathery Texture Instead of Crisp:** Adjust drying time and temperature for your specific food type.

Storage Tips for Dried Foods

Proper storage is essential to maintain flavor, texture, and safety:

- **Vacuum-Sealed Bags:** Best for long-term storage, removing air and moisture.
- **Airtight Containers:** Use glass jars or food-grade plastic containers with tight fitting lids.
- **Cool, Dark Place:** Store containers in a pantry or cupboard away from sunlight and heat.
- **Label Everything:** Always mark jars or bags with the content and drying date.

Rehydrating Dried Foods

Many dried foods can be rehydrated for cooking:

- **Fruits:** Soak in warm water for 15-30 minutes.

- **Vegetables:** Soak in water or add directly to soups and stews.
- **Mushrooms:** Soak in hot water for 20-30 minutes; use soaking water as a flavorful broth.

Rehydration can vary based on the food, so patience is key.

Energy-Efficient Drying Tips

- Dry foods during off-peak electricity hours.
- Use solar-powered dehydrators if possible.
- Always batch-process multiple trays to maximize efficiency.

When we first started drying food on our homestead, we began with sun-dried tomatoes laid out on old window screens in the sunniest spot in our garden. The smell of drying tomatoes mingling with basil from nearby herb beds became a treasured summer memory. As our homestead grew, we invested in a dehydrator, which allowed us to experiment with fruit leathers, vegetable powders, and even homemade jerky. The satisfaction of seeing neatly packed jars of dried apple chips and herb blends in our pantry is hard to describe it's like bottling summer sunshine for the colder months.

Drying is a versatile and rewarding preservation method that celebrates the essence of your harvest while providing a practical solution for food storage. Whether you embrace traditional sun-drying or opt for the precision of a modern dehydrator, the process transforms fresh produce into pantry staples that offer convenience, nutrition, and the satisfaction of homemade preservation.

Each dried piece holds the story of your garden, capturing the essence of the season in a form that can be enjoyed throughout the year.

5.4 Freeze-Drying: Taking Food Preservation to the Next Level

Freeze drying is the gold standard of food preservation. It offers unparalleled shelf life, nutrition retention, and versatility. While it's a significant investment, as freeze dryers are expensive and require space, they are an incredible tool for those ready to take their food preservation efforts to the next level. Imagine being able to preserve an entire harvest, from garden vegetables to juicy fruits, meats, and even complete meals, with their flavors, nutrients, and textures nearly perfectly intact.

At its core, freeze-drying works by freezing food at extremely low temperatures and then slowly removing moisture through a vacuum process. This method preserves up to **97% of the food's nutrients,** compared to 60-80% with traditional dehydration. The result is lightweight, long-lasting food that can be stored for **20-30 years** when properly sealed and stored in airtight containers.

Benefits of Freeze-Drying

- **Nutritional Value:** Retains nearly all vitamins and minerals.
- **Flavor and Texture:** Freeze-dried food rehydrates beautifully, often tasting as fresh as the day it was picked or cooked.
- **Shelf Life:** Properly stored freeze-dried food can last decades.
- **Versatility:** Freeze-drying works for fruits, vegetables, meats, dairy, and even full meals like soups or stews.
- **Portability:** Lightweight and easy to store, making it perfect for emergency supplies or camping trips.

Foods Ideal for Freeze-Drying

Freeze-drying works exceptionally well for a variety of foods:

- **Fruits:** Strawberries, apples, bananas, blueberries
- **Vegetables:** Peas, corn, green beans, bell peppers
- **Meats:** Cooked chicken, beef, turkey, and even raw meat for long-term storage
- **Dairy:** Milk, yogurt, cheese
- **Full Meals:** Soups, stews, pasta dishes

How Freeze-Drying Works at Home

1. **Prep the Food:** Wash, slice, or cook food as needed. Smaller pieces freeze dry faster.
2. **Load the Freeze Dryer:** Arrange food evenly on trays to ensure consistent results.
3. **Freeze Phase:** The machine freezes the food at extremely low temperatures (- 40°F).
4. **Vacuum Phase:** A vacuum removes moisture from the frozen food through sublimation (ice converts directly to vapor).
5. **Seal the Food:** Once dried, store food in mylar bags with oxygen absorbers or airtight glass jars.

Simple Freeze-Dried Snack Recipe: Strawberries

- **Ingredients:** Fresh strawberries
- **Steps:**
  1. Wash and slice strawberries evenly.
  2. Arrange on freeze-dryer trays in a single layer.
  3. Run the freeze-dryer cycle (approximately 24-36 hours, depending on moisture content).
  4. Once complete, store in airtight containers with oxygen absorbers.

These sweet and tangy strawberries are perfect for snacking, adding to cereal, or tossing into baked goods.

Freeze-drying isn't for everyone. The initial investment can be intimidating, with machines often costing **$2,000-$4,000.** Additionally, they require a dedicated space and regular maintenance. However, if you grow large amounts of food, enjoy camping or backpacking, or want to build an emergency food supply, a freeze dryer might just be your new favorite homestead tool.

Think of freeze-drying as a long-term investment. Not just in equipment, but in your family's self-sufficiency, food security, and the joy of knowing your harvest can last for decades. Whether you're preserving a summer bumper crop or preparing home-cooked meals for future convenience, freeze-drying offers a unique way to extend your food preservation toolkit.

In the end, food preservation is about finding the methods that work best for your family, your lifestyle, and your goals. Freeze-drying might be a big step, but for those ready to take it, the rewards are as lasting as the food it preserves.

5.5 Troubleshooting Preservation Challenges

As you dive into the world of food preservation, you might encounter a few bumps along the way. These challenges are part of the learning curve and can be tackled with a bit of patience and know-how. One common canning mistake is overfilling jars. It seems harmless, but it can lead to improper sealing, which risks spoilage. Always leave the recommended headspace-usually a half inch for high-acid foods and an inch for low-acid foods. This space allows for the expansion of food and the formation of a vacuum seal.

Another frequent issue is inconsistent fermentation temperatures. Fermentation thrives in a stable environment, ideally between 65°F and 75°F. Fluctuations can slow the process or encourage unwanted bacteria. Using a consistent spot in your home or investing in a fermentation heater can help maintain the right conditions.

Canning can present its own set of hurdles. A failed seal is a common problem, often due to an unclean jar rim or an improperly tightened lid. If a jar fails to seal, it's crucial to act quickly. Check for any residue on the rim, then reprocess the jar using a new lid within 24 hours. Adjusting for altitude is another critical factor. At higher altitudes, water boils at a lower temperature, which can affect processing times. You'll need to increase the processing time or pressure to ensure food safety. Consult a reliable canning guide to determine the precise adjustments for your altitude. These small tweaks can make a significant difference in the success of your canning efforts.

When it comes to fermentation, a few pitfalls can arise. Mold growth on ferments is a concern, which is often caused by exposure to air. Keeping your ferment submerged under the brine is key. If mold does appear, it's usually safe to remove it and continue fermenting, but if you notice off odors or textures, it's best to err on the side of caution and discard the batch.

Balancing flavors in fermented foods is another aspect to consider. If your ferment is too salty or sour, it might be due to an imbalance in the initial recipe. Adjusting salt levels or fermentation time in future batches can help achieve the desired taste. Sometimes, adding herbs or spices can enhance flavors, transforming a basic ferment into something extraordinary.

Drying foods has its quirks, especially in humid climates where moisture can hinder the process. Ensuring even drying is crucial to prevent spoilage. In areas with high humidity, using a food dehydrator is often the best solution. It provides consistent heat and air circulation, which helps remove moisture more effectively than air drying alone. Over-drying is another potential challenge, leading to a loss of nutrients and a less appealing texture. Monitoring drying times and checking for pliability rather than brittleness can help maintain the quality of dried foods. Properly dried food should be leathery and flexible, not crisp or brittle.

Troubleshooting these challenges is part of the evolving practice of food preservation. Each mistake offers a lesson, an opportunity to refine your techniques and deepen your understanding. As you gain experience, these challenges will become less daunting. You'll develop a knack for spotting potential issues before they escalate, turning preservation from a daunting task into a rewarding endeavor. Mastering these skills equips you to make the most of your harvest, ensuring that the fruits of your labor are preserved safely and deliciously.

In this chapter, we've explored the ins and outs of food preservation, from fermentation to canning and drying. We've navigated common pitfalls and learned how to troubleshoot them, ensuring that your efforts lead to success. These skills not only preserve your harvest but also enrich your lifestyle, offering a taste of self-sufficiency and sustainability. The journey of homesteading is about embracing challenges and finding joy in the solutions. As we move forward, we'll delve into other aspects of self-sufficient living, expanding your homesteading skills and deepening your connection to the land.

6

HARNESSING RENEWABLE ENERGY AT HOME

When we first started our homesteading adventure, the thought of powering our home with the sun seemed like a distant dream. The idea of reducing our reliance on the grid while embracing a sustainable lifestyle was appealing but intimidating. However, as I dug deeper into the world of solar energy, I discovered that this dream was more attainable than I had imagined. Solar power is not only a clean and renewable energy source but also a practical solution for anyone looking to minimize their carbon footprint and embrace self-sufficiency. Installing solar panels on your property can be a rewarding DIY project that significantly cuts energy costs and contributes to a greener planet.

Understanding the basics of solar power is the first step in making this dream a reality. At the heart of solar technology are **photovoltaic (PV) cells,** tiny units that convert sunlight into electricity. These cells are housed in solar panels, which capture solar energy and convert it into **direct current (DC) electricity.** To power your home, this DC electricity must be transformed into **alternating current (AC) electricity,** which is the type your household appliances use. This transformation is achieved through an **inverter,** a key component of any solar power system. Additionally, a **battery may be included** to store excess energy for use during cloudy days or at night, ensuring a constant power supply. Together, these components create a system that allows you to harness the power of the sun and reduce your dependence on traditional energy sources.

Assessing Your Solar Potential

Determining whether solar power is a good fit for your homestead requires careful evaluation of your energy needs and your property's sunlight exposure. Start by understanding your household's average monthly energy consumption, which is typically measured in kilowatt-hours (kWh). This information is often listed on your electricity bill, but using an energy consumption calculator can provide a more detailed breakdown of how different appliances contribute to your energy usage.

Once you have this information, you can determine the size of the solar system you'll need to meet your energy demands.

Next, analyze your property's sunlight exposure to identify the optimal placement for solar panels. Panels should ideally be installed in a location that receives full sun for most of the day, facing south in the northern hemisphere, with minimal shading from nearby trees or buildings. For a more accurate assessment, tools and resources can calculate solar potential based on roof orientation, shading, and local solar radiation data. If your area experiences frequent cloud cover or unpredictable weather, you might also consider integrating a solar battery system to store excess electricity generated during sunny periods for use when sunlight is limited. Conducting a solar site survey or measuring solar irradiance can help you maximize the efficiency of your solar setup.

Here are some helpful tools and methods to explore as you assess your solar potential:

1. Calculating Energy Consumption

Look for energy consumption calculators, which allow you to estimate your household energy usage based on appliance type and usage patterns. These calculators are often available on energy efficiency websites or through utility companies.

Refer to your monthly utility bills to find your average energy consumption, listed in kilowatt-hours (kWh).

2. Analyzing Sunlight Exposure

Google Project Sunroof and similar platforms can estimate your roof's solar potential by analyzing its orientation, shading, and sunlight availability. While these are online tools, you can consult local solar installation companies for comparable insights if you don't have internet access.

For in-depth calculations, look for regional or national solar energy organizations, which often offer guidance on assessing solar radiation and photovoltaic production potential in your area.

3. Conducting a Solar Site Survey

A solar site survey involves evaluating your property's sunlight exposure, roof orientation, and shading. This can often be done with the help of solar installers or by following solar installation guides found in books or publications about renewable energy.

Look for local workshops or community programs that teach basic solar site survey techniques.

4. Measuring Solar Irradiance

Solar irradiance measurement tools, such as handheld solar meters, can help you determine the sunlight intensity at your property. These can often be purchased or borrowed from hardware stores or solar suppliers.

Many homesteading or renewable energy books provide instructions for estimating solar irradiance manually or with basic tools.

By exploring these resources and methods, you can confidently evaluate your property's solar potential and make informed decisions about installing solar panels. Remember, your local library, renewable energy organizations, and community solar groups can also be invaluable sources of information and support for your solar journey.

Cost Breakdown Example

Switching to solar power often brings up a big question: *How much does it actually cost?* While prices vary depending on location, system size, and whether you hire a professional installer or go the DIY route, here's a general guideline:

- **DIV Solar Kit (5kW System):** Approximately **$6,000-$10,000** (including panels, inverter, and installation tools). Labor is free if you're doing it yourself, but you'll invest your time and effort.

- **Professional Installation (5kW System):** Approximately **$15,000-$25,000** (including panels, inverter, labor, and warranties).

A DIY installation can save you thousands of dollars upfront, but hiring professionals offers peace of mind, experience, and sometimes extended warranties. For many homesteaders, starting small with a few panels and gradually expanding the system over time is a reasonable approach.

Addressing Common Concerns

Switching to solar can feel like a big leap, and it's normal to have some questions. Here are answers to a few common concerns:

1. **What if I don't generate enough energy during cloudy days or winter months?** Modern solar panels are highly efficient, even on cloudy days. Additionally, investing in a good battery storage system can keep your home running smoothly during low-sunlight periods.

2. **Is solar power worth it if I don't plan to live here forever?**
   Absolutely! A solar power system can increase your property value significantly. It's considered one of the most attractive home upgrades for potential buyers.

3. **What about maintenance and repairs?**
   Solar panels are incredibly **low-maintenance.** Aside from occasional cleaning and an annual inspection, there's very little upkeep involved. Most systems come with warranties that cover defects and repairs for up to 25 years.

4. **Is solar installation safe for someone with no electrical experience?**
   If you're comfortable following step-by-step instructions and taking basic safety precautions, a DIY solar kit is manageable. However, if wiring feels intimidating, it's worth hiring an electrician for the final hookup.

Battery Systems: The Power of Energy Storage

Batteries are the unsung heroes of any solar power system. While your panels generate electricity during the day, excess energy can be stored in a battery bank for later use. This is especially helpful for nighttime power needs or for cloudy days.

Advanced storage solutions, like the Tesla Powerwall or Generac PWRcell, allow homeowners to store large amounts of energy efficiently. These batteries come with smart monitoring systems that help optimize energy use, ensuring your homestead gets the most out of every sunbeam.

If a full battery setup feels like a big investment, you can start with a smaller battery bank and expand as your budget allows. Think of it as building your homestead's energy resilience, one charge at a time.

Sustainability Benefits: A Greener Tomorrow

Every solar panel installed on your property is a step toward a cleaner planet. On average, a **SkW solar system can offset approximately 10,000 pounds of CO_2 emissions per** year-that's equivalent to planting **150 trees annually!**

Beyond environmental benefits, switching to solar reduces the strain on local power grids, especially during peak usage times. For homesteaders, this isn't just about savings or self-sufficiency; it's about being a responsible steward of the land and leaving a better world for future generations.

Interactive Element: Solar Suitability Checklist

- **Calculate Energy Needs:** Review your electricity bill for average monthly consumption.
- **Evaluate Sunlight Exposure:** Observe your property's sun patterns and identify the best panel placement.
- **Budget for Installation:** Research DIY solar kits and compare costs to estimate savings.

- **Plan Maintenance Schedule:** Set reminders for regular panel cleaning and inspections.

By understanding these core elements of solar power, you equip yourself with the knowledge to create a sustainable energy system that supports your homesteading goals.

6.2 DIY Wind Turbines for Power Generation

When people hear the term "wind energy," it often stirs a mix of reactions, especially in areas where the landscape's natural beauty is highly valued. Large-scale wind farms, with their towering turbines and blinking red lights, are often associated with industrial intrusion. But rest assured, a homestead-scale wind turbine is a completely different story.

Smaller, low-profile wind turbines are designed to blend into your property while meeting your energy needs. These systems don't dominate the skyline or disrupt the peaceful charm of rural life. Instead, they're modest, functional, and tailored to fit seamlessly within a homesteading lifestyle. The gentle hum of a small wind turbine turning in the breeze isn't just a soothing sound—it's the sound of clean, renewable energy working to power your home.

Wind energy is a fantastic complement to other renewable energy sources like solar power. While solar panels excel on sunny days, wind turbines often produce power on cloudy, breezy ones, offering a consistent energy supply in varying conditions. However, wind energy isn't ideal for every homestead. Its effectiveness depends on factors like local wind conditions, elevation, and available space. For homesteads with steady winds of at least 10–12 mph and minimal obstructions, wind turbines can be a valuable addition to energy independence.

Why DIY Wind Turbines Are Ideal for Homesteaders

1. **Energy Independence**: Wind turbines allow home-steaders to generate their own clean electricity, reducing reliance on external power sources.
2. **Scalability**: DIY turbines are smaller and more adaptable, making them a perfect fit for personal energy needs rather than the vast demands of industrial systems.
3. **Sustainability**: These turbines utilize a renewable energy source—wind—that can power homes day or night, provided there's a steady breeze.
4. **Cost-Effectiveness**: Using salvaged materials or DIY kits significantly reduces the cost of setting up a turbine compared to commercial systems.

Before deciding, evaluate your property's wind potential. Open spaces with minimal obstructions like trees or buildings work best. If you're in a region with consistent winds and have adequate space, a DIY wind turbine might be just what you need to take the next step toward sustainability.

Practical Steps to Implement DIY Wind Turbines

Building and installing your own wind turbine can be a rewarding project that combines creativity, technical skill, and a hands-on approach to renewable energy. Here's how you can start:

1. **Designing the Blades**:
   The blades are critical for efficiently capturing wind. Use lightweight, durable materials like PVC pipes, which are affordable and easy to shape. The design must ensure smooth, balanced rotation even in moderate winds.

2. **Assembling the Frame and Generator**:
   The frame, typically made of steel or aluminum, must withstand harsh weather conditions. The generator, which converts the wind's kinetic energy into electricity, can be purchased as part of a kit or salvaged from old machinery. Together, these form the heart of the turbine.

3. **Choosing the Right Location**:
   Proper placement is key to maximizing wind turbine performance. Install your turbine in an open area free of obstructions, such as trees or buildings, and consider mounting it on a tower to access higher, more consistent winds. A secure foundation ensures the structure can withstand storms and high winds.

4. **Combining with Solar Energy**:
   To create a resilient energy system, pair your wind turbine with solar panels. This hybrid setup ensures power generation regardless of weather conditions. Excess energy from both sources can be stored in batteries, providing a reliable backup when the wind isn't blowing or the sun isn't shining.

5. **Maintaining the System**:
   Like any piece of equipment, wind turbines require periodic maintenance. Regularly inspect the blades,

frame, and generator for wear or damage. Tighten loose bolts and check for misaligned blades to ensure optimal performance. Adding a monitoring system can provide real-time data on energy production and help identify issues early.

Addressing Misconceptions

Many people hesitate to consider wind energy because of common misconceptions. Unlike large industrial turbines, small-scale systems are quiet, producing only a faint hum when operational. They also require less maintenance than you might expect, especially if they're installed correctly.

Moreover, DIY wind turbines can blend into a homestead's landscape without drawing undue attention. They're compact, functional, and designed to enhance sustainability without sacrificing the natural beauty of your property.

Embracing wind energy is about more than just generating electricity—it's about tapping into a renewable resource that's been part of nature's rhythm for millennia. By capturing the power of the wind, you can reduce your reliance on conventional energy sources and create a more self-sufficient homestead. Whether you choose to combine wind energy with solar power or use it as a standalone system, a DIY wind turbine is an investment in resilience, sustainability, and a cleaner future.

Exploring renewable energy isn't always simple, but the journey is incredibly rewarding. If you're ready to harness the wind, start small, stay patient, and enjoy the process. Every breeze that passes through your fields carries the potential to power your home—you just need the right tools to catch it.

6.3 Utilizing Greywater Systems for Irrigation

In the quest for sustainability, greywater recycling stands out as a practical and ecofriendly solution. Greywater refers to the relatively clean wastewater from baths, sinks, washing machines, and other kitchen appliances-but not from toilets, which is classified as blackwater. This distinction is important because greywater can be reused for irrigation, reducing the demand for fresh water and providing valuable nutrients to plants. By diverting greywater from the sewer system, you can save water, lower utility bills, and support a healthier environment. It's a simple yet effective way to make the most of the resources available to you, turning what was once wasted into a beneficial asset for your garden.

Designing Your Greywater System

Designing a greywater system for your garden begins with iden-tifying suitable sources of greywater in your home. Bathroom sinks and showers are excellent candidates since they primarily produce water with minimal contaminants. Washing machines also generate greywater, though it's crucial to use plant-friend-ly detergents free of harmful chemicals. Once you've identified your water sources, the next step is constructing a filtration and distribution system.

A basic filtration system can be achieved with a simple setup involving a sand and gravel filter to remove larger particles. From there, the filtered greywater can be directed through a network of pipes to your garden beds. Distribution systems can be as straightforward as gravity-fed channels or more complex setups involving pumps for larger areas. The key is ensuring the system is easy to maintain, fits your specific landscape needs, and delivers water efficiently to your plants.

For a simple example, a **washing machine greywater system** can be set up using a diversion valve that routes water directly from your washing machine to nearby fruit trees or ornamental shrubs. Pairing this setup with a mulch basin-essentially a circular depression filled with mulch around each plant-encourages slow water absorption and reduces runoff.

Best Plants for Greywater Irrigation

Not all plants respond equally to greywater irrigation. Fruit trees and shrubs, with their deep roots, are ideal candidates for greywater because they are less sensitive to variations in water quality. Hardy perennials and ornamental plants also thrive under greywater systems.

Some great options include:

- **Fruit Trees:** Citrus, apple, peach, and plum trees.
- **Shrubs:** Lavender, rosemary, and sage.
- **Ornamentals:** Native drought-tolerant plants, like sunflowers or succulents.

On the other hand, plants where water directly touches edible parts, like leafy greens (e.g., lettuce, spinach, and kale), are not ideal for greywater irrigation due to potential contamination risks.

Safety and Regulations

Safety and regulations are pivotal when implementing a greywater system. It's essential to avoid contaminants that could harm plants or soil. Opt for biodegradable, non-toxic cleaning products low in sodium and boron, as these elements can accumulate in the soil and damage plant health over time.

Complying with **local greywater laws and codes** is equally important. Regulations vary by region-some areas require permits, while others have specific guidelines on how greywater can be used. Familiarize yourself with these rules to ensure your system adheres to legal standards and operates safely.

Additionally, it's wise to keep greywater away from edible parts of plants, directing it towards ornamental gardens or using it in **subsurface irrigation systems** to minimize human contact and health risks. Regularly inspect your system for blockages, leaks, or signs of contamination to maintain long-term safety and functionality.

Cost Breakdown: Basic vs. Advanced Systems

While greywater systems can save money in the long run, they do require an initial investment. A **basic greywater system,** such as routing water from a washing machine to a small grove of fruit trees, can cost between **$200-$500** if you're using DIY materials and setup. In contrast, a **more advanced system,** with filtration pumps, multiple outlets, and automated controls, may range from **$1,000-$3,000** or more, depending on the scale and complexity.

If you're on a tight budget, starting small with a manual diversion system and gradually upgrading components over time can be an effective strategy.

Maximizing Efficiency with Greywater

Maximizing irrigation efficiency with greywater involves aligning the system's output with your plants' needs. This means considering the types of plants you're watering and their water requirements.

For example, **fruit trees and shrubs** with deeper roots may benefit more from greywater irrigation than shallow-rooted vegetables. Adjusting the flow rate and timing can optimize absorption, ensuring plants receive adequate moisture without overwatering.

Incorporating **mulch basins** around your plants can further enhance soil absorption. Mulch retains moisture, reduces evaporation, and prevents runoff, making it a perfect companion for greywater systems. By creating a basin or depression around each plant and filling it with mulch, you encourage the slow release of water into the soil, allowing roots to take up moisture efficiently.

Regular **soil testing** is also important. Over time, sodium and boron from detergents can build up in the soil, impacting its health. Testing your soil annually can help you monitor these levels and adjust detergent choices or system design as needed.

Greywater Maintenance Tips

Proper maintenance ensures your greywater system remains efficient and safe for years to come. Here are a few tips to keep your system in top shape:

- **Filter Cleaning:** Regularly clean sand and gravel filters to prevent clogging.
- **Inspect Pipes:** Check for blockages or leaks in your piping network.
- **Monitor Plants:** Watch for signs of stress, like yellowing leaves or stunted growth, which may indicate water quality issues.
- **Seasonal Adjustments:** Adjust flow rates during wet or dry seasons to match changing water needs.

Greywater and Soil Health

The relationship between greywater and soil health is dynamic. While greywater provides moisture and nutrients to plants, prolonged use without monitoring can lead to soil imbalances.

Sodium buildup, for instance, can reduce soil permeability over time.

To maintain healthy soil:

- Rotate greywater application areas periodically.
- Use gypsum to counteract sodium buildup.
- Regularly add organic matter to enrich soil health.

Greywater systems offer a way to integrate sustainable practices into daily life, transforming everyday actions into meaningful contributions to environmental stewardship. They bridge the gap between resource use and conservation, emphasizing the interconnectedness of our household habits and the natural world.

This approach aligns with the principles of **permaculture,** where every element in a system serves multiple functions, creating a harmonious balance between human needs and ecological health. By embracing greywater recycling, you not only reduce your environmental impact but also foster a deeper connection to the land and its cycles.

6.4 Creating an Off-Grid Energy Plan

When considering the shift to an off-grid lifestyle, it's essential to evaluate whether this approach aligns with your goals for energy independence and self-sufficiency. Begin by reflecting on what energy independence means for you. Is it about reducing your environmental impact, cutting utility costs, or ensuring a reliable power supply in case of outages? Each goal shapes your plan differently. Once your objectives are clear, take stock of your current energy consumption patterns. Examine your electricity bills to identify peak usage times and high-energy appliances. This assessment provides a baseline for the energy capacity your off-grid system must support. It's a critical step to ensure that your system can handle your needs without leaving you in the dark. Understanding your energy habits also highlights opportunities for efficiency improvements, setting the stage for a more sustainable lifestyle.

An effective off-grid system combines several key components, each playing a vital role in maintaining a stable energy supply. At the heart of the setup is the inverter, which converts the DC electricity generated by your renewable sources into AC electricity that powers your home. The charge controller is another crucial element, as it regulates the flow of electricity to the battery bank and prevents overcharging. This not only extends the life of your batteries but also optimizes system performance.

Speaking of batteries, they serve as the backbone of any off-grid system. They store excess energy for use when the sun isn't shining, or the wind isn't blowing. Adequate battery capacity is essential to ensure you have power during low-generation periods. To enhance security and reliability, consider incorporating a backup generator. This secondary power source can provide a safety net during prolonged periods of low renewable output, offering peace of mind and continuous energy access.

Transitioning to an off-grid system isn't an overnight process. It requires a thoughtful, phased approach to ensure success. Start by prioritizing energy-saving upgrades. Simple changes like switching to LED lighting or upgrading to energy-efficient appliances can significantly reduce your overall energy demand. These improvements make your eventual off-grid system more manageable and cost-effective. With a leaner energy profile, you can begin phasing in renewable components. You might start with solar panels, adding wind turbines or other renewable sources as budget and resources allow. Each addition brings you closer to full independence. As you integrate these elements, continuously monitor your energy production and consumption, adjusting your setup to meet your evolving needs. This incremental approach not only spreads the cost over time but also allows you to refine your system based on real-world performance.

Maintaining energy independence involves regular system checks and a proactive approach to seasonal variations. Regular maintenance of your renewable components ensures they operate at peak efficiency. Check your solar panels for debris and damage, inspect wind turbines for wear, and monitor battery health to prevent unexpected failures. These routine tasks keep your system running smoothly, extending its lifespan and reliability. Additionally, adapt your energy usage to seasonal energy variations. In summer, when solar production is high, plan energy-intensive activities during daylight hours.

Conversely, in winter, conserve energy by prioritizing essential functions and relying on stored energy or backup systems. Being flexible and responsive to these fluctuations is key to maintaining a resilient off-grid lifestyle.

As you embrace this path, you'll discover that off-grid living is as much about the right mindset as it is about technology. It's about finding a balance between consumption and conservation and between independence and community. It's about understanding that every watt saved is a step towards sustainability. Your off-grid journey is a personal evolution, reflecting your values and commitment to a greener future. With each adjustment and improvement, you'll experience the satisfaction of forging a lifestyle that's not only sustainable but also empowering. Your home becomes a testament to the possibilities of renewable energy and a beacon of hope for a more sustainable world.

As we conclude our exploration of harnessing renewable energy at home, we transition into the enjoyable world of crafting and DIY projects for the homestead. Here, we'll continue to build on the principles of self-sufficiency and sustainable living, offering creative ways to enhance your homestead with your own hands. Let's get started.

7

CRAFTING AND DIY
PROJECTS FOR THE HOMESTEAD

There's something uniquely satisfying about building something with your own hands. I've had the privilege of watching my husband craft countless pieces for our homestead. From sturdy benches to open kitchen shelving and even a dry sauna off our back deck, each project reflects patience, skill, and a deep sense of care. These creations aren't just practical-they're woven into the rhythm of our daily lives, supporting everything from morning coffee on a handcrafted bench to evenings spent unwinding in the sauna.

The first part of this chapter aims to guide you through the basics of woodworking, offering insights and inspiration for building both functional and beautiful additions to your homestead. Whether you're crafting something simple like a shelf or dreaming of a more ambitious structure, woodworking is a skill that rewards both the builder and the home it serves.

Woodworking for Practical Homestead Needs

Woodworking blends creativity with practicality, making it a perfect fit for homesteaders who value both form and function. To get started, you'll need to familiarize yourself with essential tools like saws, drills, and sanders. A good saw, such as a hand saw or circular saw, is indispensable for cutting wood to size. Drills allow you to create precise holes for screws and joints, while sanders smooth out rough edges, ensuring a polished finish.

Safety should always come first. Protective gear, including goggles and hearing protection, is non-negotiable when working with power tools. Keeping your workspace organized and free of hazards prevents accidents and allows you to focus on your project. Understanding the basics of tool maintenance is also vital. A sharp saw and a well maintained drill are not only safer but also make the work easier and more enjoyable.

Once you've familiarized yourself with the tools and safety practices, you'll be ready to tackle your first project. Raised garden beds are an excellent starting point. Begin with untreated wood like cedar or redwood, which naturally resists rot and pests. Measure and cut your boards, assemble them using screws and a drill, and voila-you've built a structure that improves drainage, makes gardening more accessible, and looks beautiful in your outdoor space.

Another practical project is a compost bin. A simple three-bin design allows for easy rotation and aeration, speeding up the composting process. It's an efficient way to turn kitchen scraps and yard waste into nutrient-rich soil while keeping your homestead tidy and sustainable.

Beyond Utility: Building for Comfort and Character

Some of my favorite pieces on our homestead are the ones my husband built not out of necessity, but from a vision of making our space more comfortable and inviting. The open kitchen shelving he installed doesn't just hold our jars and dishes-it brings warmth and character to the heart of our home.

Furniture projects like a simple wooden bench or a custom-built table can be deeply satisfying to create. Even if you're just beginning, these projects don't have to be overly complicated. Start with reclaimed or locally sourced wood, which often brings its own story to the project. Each cut, sanding pass, and coat of stain transforms raw material into something personal and enduring.

Custom shelves are another approachable project. Whether you're fitting them into a corner of your home office or building a display for family heirlooms, they can be tailored to your exact needs and space. The beauty of building your own shelves is in the flexibility-they can be as simple or as elaborate as your time, budget, and skill allow.

If you're feeling ambitious, larger projects like outdoor furniture or a small sauna can elevate your space in remarkable ways. Building these takes more planning and patience, but the end result is deeply rewarding. A sauna, for example, offers not just a space for relaxation but also a tangible reflection of the effort and care that went into its creation.

Finishing Touches: Staining, Sealing, and Maintenance

The final step of any woodworking project is often the most transformative. Sanding is where the wood starts to come to life, revealing its natural grain and texture. Start with coarse sandpaper to smooth out imperfections, then gradually move to finer grits for a polished surface.

Staining adds warmth and personality to your project. Choose a stain that complements your space and apply it evenly with a brush or cloth, following the direction of the wood grain. Once the stain has dried, sealing is essential to protect the wood from moisture, wear, and weather exposure. Products like polyurethane, tung oil, or beeswax finishes are popular choices, each offering different levels of protection and sheen.

Regular maintenance, such as reapplying sealants and checking for signs of weather damage, ensures your projects stay beautiful and functional for years to come.

Your First Woodworking Project: A Simple Bench

If you're ready to start small but meaningful, a basic wooden bench is the perfect introduction to woodworking.

Materials You'll Need:

- Untreated cedar or pine boards
- Wood screws
- Sandpaper (coarse and fine grit)
- Stain or sealant
- Drill and drill bits
- Circular saw or hand saw

Steps to Build Your Bench:

1. **Measure and Cut the Wood:** Cut two long boards for the seat and two shorter boards for the legs.
2. **Assemble the Frame:** Attach the legs to the seat using wood screws, making sure everything is level and sturdy.
3. **Sand the Surfaces:** Smooth out rough edges and surfaces with sandpaper.
4. **Stain and Seal:** Apply your chosen stain and let it dry before sealing the wood for durability.

In just a few hours, you'll have a sturdy, beautiful bench ready to use on your porch, in your garden, or next to a cozy firepit.

Woodworking isn't just about building things-it's about the stories each piece carries. Whether it's a bench for morning coffee, open shelving in the kitchen, or a sauna where the day melts away, every creation becomes a lasting part of your homestead's story.

You don't have to be an expert to start. Every project, no matter how small, teaches you something valuable. Over time, those lessons add up, and you'll find yourself tackling larger, more ambitious builds with confidence.

So, whether you're assembling your first compost bin or crafting a one-of-a-kind dining table, embrace the process. Take your time, learn from your mistakes, and celebrate every completed project. There's nothing quite like standing back, admiring your handiwork, and knowing you built it with your own two hands.

Crafting Herbal Remedies from Your Garden

Embracing the power of nature through herbal remedies is like tapping into an ancient wisdom that's both healing and nurturing. On our homestead, the garden serves as both a source of nourishment and a natural pharmacy. Selecting medicinal herbs to grow is the first step in crafting remedies that align with these traditions. Chamomile, with its gentle, calming properties, is a favorite for promoting relaxation and easing digestive discomfort. Its daisy-like flowers are as charming as they are useful. Lavender, known for its soothing scent, supports calmness and can also aid in treating minor skin irritations. Echinacea, often called the coneflower, is prized for its immune-boosting qualities, making it a staple during cold and flu season. Companion planting these herbs not only enhances their growth by creating a supportive plant community but also enriches the biodiversity of your garden, encouraging beneficial insects and improving soil health.

Once your herbs are thriving, knowing when and how to harvest them is key to preserving their potency. Timing is everything; for most herbs, the best time to harvest is in the morning after the dew has dried but before the sun is too high. This is when the essential oils are most concentrated. Snip the herbs with sharp scissors or pruning shears to avoid damaging the plant.

Drying is a traditional method of preservation that maintains the integrity of the herbs over time. Hang small bunches upside down in a warm, airy place away from direct sunlight.

This process allows them to retain their color and flavor. Once dry, store them in airtight containers, keeping them cool and dark to prevent degradation.

Making tinctures is another effective way to capture the essence of your herbs. By steeping the herbs in alcohol or vinegar, you extract their medicinal constituents, creating a potent liquid remedy that can be stored for extended periods. This method is particularly useful for herbs like echinacea and valerian, whose active compounds are best preserved in liquid form.

Creating herbal remedies at home opens up a world of possibilities for addressing common ailments naturally. Herbal teas are a gentle and effective way to enjoy the benefits of your garden-grown herbs. For relaxation and digestion, a blend of chamomile and peppermint makes a soothing evening drink. Simply steep the dried herbs in hot water, strain, and savor the calming effects.

Herbal salves are invaluable for topical applications. Combining calendula and lavender in a beeswax-based salve creates a healing balm for minor cuts, burns, and dry skin.

Gently melt beeswax and a carrier oil, like olive or almond oil, over low heat. Add the herbs, then strain and pour the mixture into small jars to cool. These homemade remedies provide a natural first aid kit right from your own garden.

Safety and responsible use are paramount when working with herbal remedies. Understanding recommended dosages is crucial, as herbs, while natural, can still have potent effects. Start with small amounts and observe how your body responds. Remember that interactions can occur, especially if you're taking other medications. Consult with a healthcare provider if you're uncertain. Educate yourself about each herb's properties, potential side effects, and contraindications. Resources like herbal medicine books and reputable online sources can be invaluable in building your knowledge base. Always err on the side of caution, respecting the power of plants and their role in your well-being.

Interactive Element: Herbal Remedy Reflection Section

Take a moment to reflect on how you might incorporate herbal remedies into your daily life. Consider these questions:

- Which medicinal herbs are you most interested in growing and why?
- How might these herbs address specific health needs for you or your family?
- What steps can you take to ensure safe and effective use of herbal remedies?

Write down your thoughts and plans. This reflection can help you focus your efforts and create a personalized approach to herbal medicine, guided by the bounty of your garden.

Upcycling Household Items

Upcycling is a creative and meaningful way to breathe new life into items that might otherwise end up in a landfill. It's about seeing the potential in what others might consider waste, transforming the ordinary into the extraordinary. By repurposing materials, you can reduce environmental impact, exercise your creativity, and foster a more sustainable lifestyle. Each upcycling project you complete not only diverts waste from landfills but also lessens the demand for new goods, reducing the strain on natural resources and minimizing air and water pollution.

Why Upcycling Matters Imagine transforming a glass jar destined for the recycling bin into a charming herb container or converting old fabric scraps into a vibrant patchwork tote bag. These acts of transformation represent a sustainable mindset that values innovation, creativity, and environmental stewardship. Every upcycled item carries a story—a testament to the power of imagination and the joy of turning something old into something cherished.

Endless Creative Possibilities The beauty of upcycling lies in its versatility and accessibility. Here are some ideas to get you started:

- **Glass Jars:** Turn them into herb storage containers, painted vases, or candle holders.
- **Tin Cans:** Create rustic planters, utensil holders, or lanterns for your garden.
- **Old Clothes:** Transform fabric into reusable shopping bags, patchwork quilts, or even braided rugs.
- **Wine Corks:** Craft a unique bulletin board, coasters, or keychains.
- **Wooden Pallets:** Build garden shelves, vertical planters, or outdoor furniture.
- **Magazines and Paper:** Fold them into DIY envelopes, scrapbook pages, or decoupage projects.
- **Broken Ceramics:** Use them to create mosaic designs on pots, tables, or walkways.

Tools and Techniques for Upcycling To start upcycling, equip yourself with a few basic tools:

- **For Fabric Projects:** Sewing kits, needles, threads, scissors, and fabric glue are essential.
- **For Harder Materials:** Paints, brushes, adhesives, sandpaper, and small power tools.
- **Decorative Techniques:** Decoupage, distressing, and stenciling can elevate simple projects.

These tools allow you to adapt materials creatively, whether painting wooden pallets for a rustic look or stitching worn clothes into reusable totes.

Practical Tips for Success

- **Start Small:** Begin with easy projects to build your confidence and skills.
- **Look Around Your Home:** Identify items that could serve a new purpose, like repurposing a stack of old books into a unique side table.
- **Combine Materials:** Experiment with mixing wood, fabric, and glass for multi-functional designs.
- **Document Your Projects:** Take photos and notes to capture your progress and inspire future ideas.

Inspiration Chart: Materials and Project Ideas Here's a quick reference guide to spark creativity:

Material	Upcycling Ideas	Tools Needed	Techniques
Glass jars	Herb storage, candle holders, painted vases	Paint, brushes, twine	Painting, decoupage, twine-wrapping
Tin cans	Planters, utensil holders, garden lanterns	Paint, hammer, nails	Punch-hole designs, painting
Old clothes	Tote bags, quilts, braided rugs	Sewing kit, scissors, fabric glue	Stitching, patchwork

Wooden pallets	Garden shelves, furniture, vertical planters	Sandpaper, paint, screws	Sanding, painting, assembling
Wine corks	Bulletin boards, coasters, keychains	Glue, utility knife	Arranging, adhering
Broken ceramics	Mosaic pots, tables, garden paths	Grout, adhesive, trowel	Mosaic assembly
Magazines/paper	DIY envelopes, scrapbook art, decoupage	Scissors, adhesive	Folding, gluing, layering

Making a Difference Upcycling is more than a creative outlet—it's a lifestyle shift that challenges us to rethink waste and embrace resourcefulness. By approaching everyday items with fresh eyes, you can find endless possibilities for transformation. Each project, whether simple or intricate, contributes to a healthier planet and showcases the power of ingenuity.

As you explore the art of upcycling, share your creations with friends, family, and your community. Whether through social media or workshops, your projects can inspire others to rethink waste and join in the upcycling movement.

Handmade Soaps and Natural Cleaners

In a world full of synthetic chemicals, the allure of natural cleaning products is undeniable. Imagine walking into a room and inhaling the subtle, refreshing aroma of citrus or lavender, knowing that the air is free from harsh, artificial fragrances. Making your own soaps and cleaners not only reduces your exposure to chemicals but also offers peace of mind. These homemade alternatives are cost-effective, allowing you to save money while ensuring a healthier home environment. By swapping out conventional products for those you've crafted yourself, you take a significant step toward minimizing chemical exposure.

This shift can have profound effects on personal health, reducing the risk of allergies and skin irritations. Moreover, the process of crafting these products is empowering transforming raw, natural ingredients into effective cleaning solutions that leave your home sparkling and fresh.

Creating natural soap at home is a blend of chemistry and creativity. The cold process method is a traditional technique that involves combining fats-like olive or coconut oil-with lye, a substance that transforms oils into soap through saponification. While lye requires careful handling, following safety precautions ensures a smooth process and a quality end product. The magic happens as you mix the oils and lye, watching them blend into a creamy batter that will eventually harden into soap. Essential oils, such as lavender, peppermint, or eucalyptus, add fragrance and therapeutic benefits, turning each bar into a sensory delight. These oils can also provide skin-loving properties, making your soap not only cleansing but nourishing. Once poured into molds, the soap takes several weeks to cure, during which time it hardens and becomes mild enough for use. This patience is rewarded with bars that lather beautifully and leave skin feeling soft and clean.

Simple Homemade Soap Recipe Ingredients:

- 16 oz olive oil
- 8 oz coconut oil
- 4 oz lye (sodium hydroxide)
- 10 oz distilled water
- 10-15 drops essential oil (e.g., lavender, peppermint, or eucalyptus)

Instructions:

1. In a large heat-safe container, carefully mix the **lye** with **distilled water** (always add lye to water, never the other way around).
2. In a separate container, combine the **olive oil** and **coconut oil.**
3. Once both mixtures are at a similar temperature **(100-110°F),** slowly pour the **lye water** into the **oils** while stirring continuously.
4. Stir until the mixture reaches **trace** (a pudding-like consistency).
5. Add **essential oils** and stir well.
6. Pour the soap mixture into a **mold** and smooth the surface.
7. Let the soap sit in the mold for **24-48 hours.**
8. Once firm, remove it from the mold, cut it into **bars,** and let it **cure for 4-6 weeks** in a well-ventilated space.

This simple soap recipe is a great starting point, yielding bars that are gentle on the skin and naturally fragrant with your chosen essential oils.

Crafting natural cleaners with everyday ingredients is surprisingly simple and effective. Vinegar and baking soda form the backbone of many homemade cleaning solutions, their abilities to cut through grease and neutralize odors making them invaluable allies. A solution of vinegar and water works wonders on glass surfaces, leaving them streak-free and gleaming. For a deeper clean, sprinkle baking soda on surfaces before spraying with vinegar to create a fizzy reaction that lifts grime and dirt. Citrus-based disinfectants are another powerful option, harnessing the natural antibacterial properties of lemons and oranges. Simply infuse vinegar with citrus peels for a few weeks, then strain and use as an all-purpose cleaner. This not only cleans but also infuses your home with the bright, uplifting scent of citrus.

All-Purpose Natural Spray Cleaner Recipe

- **Ingredients:**
  - ❑ 1 cup distilled white vinegar
  - ❑ 1 cup water
  - ❑ 10 drops essential oil (e.g., lemon, lavender, or tea tree)

- **Instructions:**

  1. Combine the vinegar, water, and essential oil in a clean spray bottle.
  2. Shake gently to mix the ingredients.
  3. Spray on countertops, glass, or bathroom surfaces, and wipe clean with a soft cloth.

This cleaner is versatile and effective and leaves your home smelling naturally fresh.

On our homestead, we use doTERRA essential oils because we believe in their exceptional quality. However, there are many other reputable brands available, and it's worth taking the time to research and find one that aligns with your values and needs. Essential oils not only add delightful fragrances to your cleaning products and soaps but also offer added benefits, such as their antibacterial, antifungal, and mood-boosting properties.

Once you've crafted your soaps and cleaners, thoughtful packaging and storage can enhance both their functionality and appeal. Reusable containers like glass jars or spray bottles are perfect for storing your creations, reducing waste, and keeping products fresh. Labeling each container with its contents and date of creation ensures you can easily identify and track your products. For those who enjoy sharing their creations, home-made soaps make delightful gifts. Wrap them in pretty paper, or fabric, and tie them with twine or ribbon for a personal touch. A handwritten note detailing the soap's ingredients and bene-fits adds a special touch, turning a simple gift into a thoughtful gesture. Not only do these gifts reflect your creativity and care, but they also introduce others to the joys of natural products.

By embracing these practices, you not only enhance your homestead but also contribute to a healthier planet and a more intentional way of living. The satisfaction of creating something both beautiful and practical is immense. With each project, you gain skills that bolster your self-sufficiency, empowering you to make informed choices about the products you use and the impact they have. As we wrap up this chapter on crafting and DIY projects, let's look forward to exploring how these skills can further enrich your self-sufficient lifestyle in the upcoming chapters.

8

HEALTH, NUTRITION, AND WELLNESS AT HOME

Imagine biting into a tomato so rich in flavor it seems to burst with sunshine. That first taste of homegrown produce can be a revelation. When we grow our own food, we tap into nature's abundance and discover the profound difference in nutrient density compared to store-bought alternatives. The journey from garden to table is a short one, preserving the vitamins and minerals that often degrade during prolonged transit and storage. By harvesting and consuming produce at its peak ripeness, we enjoy the full spectrum of nutrients nature intended. This immediacy ensures that the food retains its nutritional potency, offering more than just sustenance but a pathway to vibrant health.

Growing your produce allows you to control soil quality and fertilization methods, sidestepping the pitfalls of conventionally grown foods, which can be laden with chemical residues. By nurturing your soil with organic matter, you create an environment where plants can thrive without the artificial boost of chemical fertilizers. This approach not only enhances the flavor and texture of your produce but also ensures that it is free from harmful contaminants. The result is a crop that is rich in phytonutrients, antioxidants, and micronutrients, compounds that support your overall well-being and protect against chronic diseases. Dr. Earth emphasizes that organic gardening leads to healthier plants that naturally deter pests, eliminating the need for chemical pesticides. This means your homegrown produce is as safe as it is delicious.

Eating seasonally aligns your diet with the natural growing cycles of fruits and vegetables, offering a host of benefits for your health and the environment. Seasonally available produce is often more nutrient-dense and flavorful, as it is harvested at its peak and requires minimal transportation and storage. This practice supports local farmers and reduces the carbon footprint associated with long-distance food transport. As you explore the bounty of each season, you invite a diverse array of flavors and nutrients into your diet. This variety not only enhances your meals but also provides a broader spectrum of vitamins and minerals essential for optimal health. Seasonal eating encourages culinary creativity, as you experiment with new recipes and discover the unique tastes of each harvest.

Maximizing nutrient retention begins with harvesting produce at its peak ripeness, a practice that ensures the highest levels of vitamins and minerals. Timing is everything. Pick your fruits and vegetables when they are fully mature, as this is when they contain the most nutrients. For example, tomatoes ripened on the vine are richer in vitamin C and lycopene than those picked early and ripened artificially. Once harvested, how you store your produce can significantly impact its nutritional value. Short-term storage solutions, such as refrigeration for leafy greens or root cellars for hardy vegetables, can help maintain freshness. Use breathable bags or perforated containers to prevent moisture buildup, which can lead to spoilage. By preserving the nutritional integrity of your produce, you ensure that each bite is as nourishing as it is enjoyable.

Choosing the right varieties can further enhance the health benefits of your homegrown produce. Certain types of kale, for instance, are packed with vitamins A, C, and K, as well as calcium, making them a powerhouse for bone health and immune support. Spinach, meanwhile, offers a different profile, rich in iron and folate, vital for energy production and DNA synthesis. Heirloom tomatoes are not just a feast for the eyes with their vibrant colors and unique shapes; they are also brimming with antioxidants like lycopene and beta carotene, compounds that support heart health and protect against oxidative stress. By selecting varieties known for their exceptional nutritional profiles, you tailor your garden to meet your health goals.

Produce	Peak Harvest Season	Key Nutrients	Storage Method
Tomatoes	Summer	Vitamin C, Lycopene	Room temperature, then refrigerate ripe tomatoes
Kale	Fall, Winter	Vitamins A, C, K, Calcium	Refrigerate in breathable bag
Spinach	Spring, Fall	Iron, Folate, Vitamin C	Refrigerate in airtight container
Carrots	Fall, Winter	Beta-Carotene, Vitamin A	Store in a root cellar or refrigerate in perforated bag
Strawberries	Spring, Early Summer	Vitamin C, Antioxidants	Refrigerate in single layer
Pumpkins	Fall	Vitamin A, Fiber	Cool, dry storage area
Peppers	Summer, Early Fall	Vitamin C, Antioxidants	Refrigerate in crisper drawer
Garlic	Summer, Fall	Allicin, Antioxidants	Store in a cool, dry, dark place
Apples	Fall	Fiber, Vitamin C	Store in a cool, dark place or refrigerator
Blueberries	Summer	Antioxidants, Vitamin C	Refrigerate in shallow container

Take a few moments to consider how your garden can support your health objectives. Reflect on these questions:

- Which nutrients are most important to your diet, and how can your garden help provide them?
- Are there specific varieties you'd like to grow to enhance your meals' nutritional value?
- How can you adjust your gardening practices to maximize nutrient retention?

Write down your thoughts and revisit them as you plan your garden. This reflection can guide your decisions, ensuring your garden becomes a cornerstone of your wellness journey.

8.2 Cooking with Fresh Ingredients: Recipes and Tips

Imagine walking into your kitchen, the air scented with the freshness of basil, the earthy undertones of tomatoes, and the crispness of just-picked greens. Cooking with ingredients straight from your garden transforms meals into something extraordinary. Fresh herbs, like rosemary and thyme, can elevate a dish's flavor profile without the need for excessive salt. A sprinkle of chopped parsley or a handful of mint can breathe new life into a simple dish, making it both nutritious and delicious. Incorporating a variety of vegetables ensures that meals are not only balanced but vibrant. Think of a plate brimming with the colors of the rainbow-deep greens, rich reds, and bright yellows. This isn't just about aesthetics; it's about creating meals that nourish the body and delight the senses.

Consider a garden vegetable stir-fry. It's a simple yet effective way to make the most of your produce. Start with a base of onions and garlic, sauteed in a splash of olive oil until translucent. Add sliced bell peppers, zucchini, and carrots, letting them sizzle and release their natural sweetness. Toss in a handful of snow peas and a sprinkle of sesame seeds for texture. Finish with a dash of soy sauce or tamari and a generous handful of fresh basil or cilantro. This dish is quick to prepare, rich in nutrients, and a testament to the power of homegrown food. Pairing it with a fresh herb salad is another delightful option. Mix a variety of greens-perhaps some arugula, spinach, and kale-with a selection of herbs like dill, parsley, and mint. Drizzle with a homemade vinaigrette made from olive oil, apple cider vinegar, a touch of mustard, and a pinch of salt and pepper. The result is a refreshing salad that complements any meal and highlights the natural flavors of your garden.

Preserving nutrients during cooking is key to maintaining the health benefits of fresh produce. Steaming is one of the best methods, as it retains the vitamins and minerals often lost through boiling. By gently steaming vegetables, you preserve their vibrant colors and firm textures, making them a joy to eat. Sauteing with healthy oils, such as olive or avocado oil, is another excellent technique. These oils not only add flavor but also help in the absorption of fat-soluble vitamins present in the vegetables. The key is to cook over medium heat, allowing the flavors to meld without compromising the nutritional value.

These methods ensure that your meals are not only tasty but also packed with the nutrients your body craves.

Embracing the seasons in your cooking allows you to enjoy the freshest produce and adapt recipes to what nature provides. In the summer, a light pasta tossed with zucchini ribbons and fresh basil captures the essence of the season. A splash of lemon juice and a sprinkle of parmesan complete the dish, bringing out the flavors of the ingredients. As the year turns to autumn, root vegetables come into their own. Roasting them enhances their natural sweetness, turning parsnips, carrots, and beets into a hearty meal. Add a drizzle of honey and a sprinkle of thyme before roasting for an extra layer of flavor. These dishes not only celebrate the season but also connect you to the cycle of growth and harvest.

Quick Recipe: Summer Zucchini Pasta

- 2 medium zucchinis, spiralized or sliced into thin ribbons

- 1 cup cherry tomatoes, halved
- 2 tbsp olive oil
- 1 tbsp lemon juice
- 1/4 cup grated parmesan cheese
- Handful of fresh basil leaves
- Salt and pepper to taste

Instructions:

1. Heat olive oil in a skillet over medium heat.
2. Add cherry tomatoes and cook until softened.
3. Add zucchini ribbons and saute for 2-3 minutes.
4. Remove from heat, add lemon juice, and sprinkle with parmesan and fresh basil.
5. Season with salt and pepper. Serve immediately.

Cooking with fresh ingredients is more than just a culinary choice; it's a commitment to health, flavor, and sustainability. Each meal becomes a reflection of your garden's bounty, a testament to the care and attention you've given to your plants. The connection between the garden and the table is a powerful one, rooted in the understanding that the best food comes from the land, nurtured by your hands. By focusing on fresh, seasonal ingredients and preserving their natural goodness, you create meals that are as nourishing as they are delicious, bringing the joy of the garden into your daily life.

8.3 Natural Remedies for Common Ailments

In a world full of quick fixes and synthetic solutions, turning to plants for healing feels like a return to something pure and genuine. Imagine the soothing power of a cup of chamomile tea, calming frazzled nerves after a long day. Chamomile, with its delicate blossoms, has been cherished for centuries for its calming properties. It works by gently relaxing the mind and body, making it a wonderful remedy for stress or insomnia.

Peppermint, with its invigorating aroma, is another garden gem. A simple peppermint infusion can ease digestive discomfort, offering relief from bloating or indigestion. The menthol in peppermint acts as a natural antispasmodic, soothing the muscles of the digestive tract.

These plants, growing quietly in your garden, hold the keys to simple but effective remedies that can support your well-being.

Crafting your own remedies can be empowering. It connects you to the healing traditions of countless generations before us. Take ginger tea, for example. With its warming qualities, it's a trusted ally against nausea and an upset stomach. Simply slice fresh ginger root and steep it in hot water. Add a touch of honey for sweetness and drink it slowly. This tea not only calms the stomach but also invigorates the senses. Similarly, honey and lemon syrup is a classic for soothing sore throats. Mix freshly squeezed lemon juice with raw honey and sip the syrup to coat and comfort your throat. These remedies are not just about alleviating symptoms; they're about taking a moment to care for yourself, using ingredients you know and trust.

Quick Herbal Remedy Reference Guide:

- **Sore Throat:** Honey and lemon syrup (1 tbsp raw honey+ juice of 1 lemon)
- **Nausea:** Ginger tea (3-4 slices fresh ginger root steeped in hot water)
- **Digestive Discomfort:** Peppermint tea (fresh peppermint leaves steeped for 5-10
- minutes)
- **Stress Relief:** Chamomile tea (2 tsp dried chamomile flowers steeped in hot water)

When using natural remedies, it's important to consider safety and efficacy. While herbs are generally safe, they can interact with medications or exacerbate certain health conditions. It's wise to consult with a healthcare professional, especially if you're pregnant, nursing, or on medication.

Understanding appropriate dosages is equally crucial. While chamomile tea is gentle enough for daily use, more potent herbs should be used with care. Keep in mind that natural doesn't always mean harmless, and respect the power of plants as you would any other medicine. Education is your best defense against unintended side effects.

Building a home apothecary is a delightful way to integrate natural remedies into your life. Start by organizing a space in your kitchen or pantry where you can store dried herbs and tinctures. Airtight glass jars are perfect for preserving the potency of your herbs, keeping them fresh and free from moisture. Label each jar with the herb name and date of harvest, so you always know what you have on hand. A remedy journal can be a valuable tool, allowing you to track the effects of different remedies and note any personal observations. This practice not only helps you refine your approach over time but also deepens your connection to the plants you grow and the remedies you create.

As you explore the world of herbal medicine, remember that the process is as much about discovery as it is about healing. Each plant offers a unique set of properties, and experimenting with combinations can be both fun and enlightening. Let your garden become a place of healing, where the plants you tend offer their gifts in return.

8.4 Incorporating Mindfulness into Homesteading

In the hustle of daily life, it's easy to get swept away by endless to-do lists and responsibilities. But bringing mindfulness into your homesteading practices can transform the way you engage with your environment, making each task more meaningful and rewarding. Imagine starting your day in the garden, not rushing through chores but truly observing the subtle changes in your plants. Notice the new buds on the tomato vines and the way the dew clings to the leaves in the early morning light. These moments of observation connect you to the present, fostering a deep appreciation for the life you nurture. Engage your senses-feel the soil between your fingers, inhale the earthy scent of growing things, and listen to the bees as they flit from flower to flower. This sensory engagement not only enriches your gardening experience but also grounds you, providing clarity and calm in the midst of life's chaos.

When you move into the kitchen, let mindfulness guide you there as well. Cooking becomes more than a necessity; it becomes a celebration of the fruits of your labor. As you prepare a meal, take the time to savor the flavors and textures of each ingredient. Notice how the sweetness of a homegrown carrot differs from its store-bought counterpart, or how the herbs you picked just moments ago infuse a dish with freshness. Practicing gratitude for each element of your meal deepens your connection to your food and the effort it took to grow it. This gratitude transforms meals into a ritual, a time to reflect on the bounty of your homestead and the simple joys it brings to your table.

Mindfulness doesn't stop at the garden or kitchen-it extends to the spaces you create around your homestead. Consider designing small areas that encourage peace and reflection. A shaded bench under your favorite tree can become a sanctuary for quiet contemplation. Use natural materials like stones, wood, and plants to create a simple yet calming atmosphere. A small meditation and prayer space tucked away among the trees, or a cozy reading nook bathed in natural light, can offer a retreat from the busyness of the day. These spaces don't need to be elaborate; their value lies in the intention behind them-a place where you can pause, breathe, and reconnect with yourself.

Balancing productivity with mindfulness is key to maintaining a fulfilling homesteading lifestyle. It's easy to fall into the trap of rushing through tasks, driven by the desire to check items off a list. However, setting clear intentions before starting each task can shift your mindset. Ask yourself: *What do I hope to accomplish with this task? How do I want to feel while doing it?* This approach helps you stay present and enjoy the process rather than simply focusing on the end result. At the end of the day, take a moment to reflect on what went well and where you might improve. These small pauses for reflection ensure that your homesteading journey is productive and aligned with your values and sense of purpose.

Incorporating mindfulness into daily tasks can turn even mundane chores into meaningful experiences. Whether you're watering plants, feeding animals, or chopping vegetables, approach each activity with a sense of presence and appreciation. Pay attention to the details: the texture of the leaves, the rhythm of your movements, or the sound of running water. These small moments of awareness add up, creating a lifestyle that feels balanced, intentional, and deeply fulfilling.

Mindful Morning Ritual Example:

- Start your day with a few moments of quiet prayer in the garden or by a window.
- Take three deep breaths, focusing on the sights, sounds, and smells around you.
- Set an intention for the day: *What do you want to focus on? How do you want to feel by the end of the day?*
- As you do your tasks, pause occasionally to check in with yourself and reset your focus if needed.

Mindfulness in homesteading isn't about slowing down for the sake of it-it's about fully inhabiting each moment, finding joy in simple tasks, and nurturing a sense of gratitude for the land and life you're building. Each day presents an opportunity to reconnect with our creator, nature, and yourself, to find peace in the rhythm of daily routines. By infusing your homestead with mindfulness, you're not just creating a productive space; you're creating a life that feels intentional, balanced, and deeply rewarding.

9

BUILDING COMMUNITY AND SHARING RESOURCES

Stepping into the world of homesteading often brings with it a mix of excitement and uncertainty. I remember the early days on our 10-acre plot-so much land, so many projects, and so many questions. While I loved the freedom and peace our homestead offered, I quickly realized I longed for something more: connection. I wanted people around me who understood this lifestyle, who could offer advice when I felt unsure, and encouragement when things didn't go as planned. Homesteading is deeply personal, but it thrives in community. This chapter is about finding your people-those who understand the joys and challenges of this lifestyle and who can offer a helping hand or a word of advice when you're knee-deep in a project.

I'll never forget when we brought home our milk cow, a beautiful Jersey. We were so excited, but I had no idea how much milk a Jersey cow produces right after calving. I didn't realize I needed to start milking her immediately, even if the calf was nursing. Within a few days, I noticed her teats becoming incredibly full, hard, and warm. Panic started to set in as I realized something was seriously wrong, and she could possibly have mastitis.

In desperation, I called a dear friend who also had a family milk cow. Without hesitation, she jumped in her car and drove 30 minutes to our home in the late evening to help me. She coached me through hand milking, encouraging me to get as much milk out as I could. But despite my best efforts, it wasn't enough. The situation was becoming more urgent, and I knew I needed additional help.

That's when I reached out to another friend who had just purchased a milking machine for her cow. Without hesitation, she and her husband loaded up the machine and drove it over to our homestead. Together, we assembled it, and for the first time, we were able to fully empty our cow's udder. That machine and the support of our friends saved us. It allowed us to get our cow back on track and eventually transition back to hand-milking.

That experience was a turning point for me. It was a reminder that while homesteading is often about self-sufficiency, we cannot-and should not-do it alone. Community means showing up for one another in moments of need, sharing tools and knowledge, and offering encouragement when things feel overwhelming. The help we received during that time meant the world to us, and it's a lesson I carry with me every day: the strength of a homesteading community lies not just in shared resources, but in shared kindness and trust.

This chapter explores how to build those connections, whether through local homesteading groups, online communities, or simple neighborly exchanges. When we lean on one another, we don't just grow stronger individually-we build a more resilient and supportive homesteading network for everyone involved.

Finding Local Homesteading Groups

Finding a local homesteading group might seem daunting at first, especially if you're new to an area or just starting on your homesteading path. But these connections are invaluable, offering support, shared resources, and a sense of belonging. Start by utilizing community bulletin boards and local newspapers. These traditional methods may seem old-fashioned, but they're often treasure troves of information about gatherings and local clubs. Farmers' markets and agricultural fairs are also fantastic places to meet people. As you stroll through stalls of fresh produce and handmade goods, strike up conversations. Ask vendors if they know of any local groups; they're usually well-connected within the community and can point you in the right direction. These events not only introduce you to potential friends but also immerse you in the local agricultural scene, giving you a taste of what your area has to offer.

Being part of a local homesteading community opens up a world of benefits. There's the obvious advantage of access to shared tools and equipment, which can save you both money and space. But beyond the tangible, there's the wealth of knowledge and skills that each member brings to the table. Perhaps someone in the group is an expert in beekeeping, while another excels in canning. These skill-sharing opportunities are priceless, allowing you to learn hands-on from those who've walked the path before you. You'll find that these communities are vibrant with ideas and experiences, fostering an environment where learning is both mutual and continuous. As you contribute your own skills and knowledge, you'll also build a network of support that can help you navigate the ups and downs of homesteading life.

Approaching a homesteading group as a newcomer can be a little intimidating, but with the right mindset, it becomes an enriching experience. Start by preparing an introductory pitch that succinctly shares your background, interests, and what you hope to learn or contribute. This doesn't have to be formal; think of it as a way to share your story. Attend group activities and events with an open mind and a willingness to volunteer.

Whether it's helping to set up for a meeting or offering to host a workshop, your involvement signals your commitment and enthusiasm. Remember, these groups thrive on the participation of their members, and your proactive engagement can forge meaningful connections.

If you find that there isn't a suitable group nearby, consider creating your own. This process begins with setting clear goals and objectives for the group. What do you hope to achieve? Is it primarily social, educational, or a mix of both? Once you have a vision, organize initial meetings to gauge interest and gather like-minded individuals. Use flyers, social media, and word-of-mouth to spread the word. Establishing a communication plan is crucial for keeping everyone informed and engaged. Consider using email lists or group messaging apps to streamline communication. As your group grows, so too will the potential for collaborative projects and shared achievements, enriching your homesteading journey and building a community united by a shared passion for sustainable living.

Community Networking Checklist

- **Identify Local Resources:** Use bulletin boards and newspapers and attend farmers' markets.
- **Engage Actively:** Prepare an introduction, volunteer for activities, and share your skills.
- **Create Your Group:** Set clear goals, organize initial meetings, and establish a communication plan.

By engaging with local homesteading groups, you not only gain practical resources and knowledge but also form bonds that enhance your connection to the community and the land.

Online Networking for Homesteaders

In today's digital age, the internet has become a powerful tool for connecting with fellow homesteaders around the globe. Social media platforms offer a gateway to vibrant communities where ideas, experiences, and encouragement are shared freely. Facebook, for instance, hosts numerous groups dedicated to homesteading, ranging from general discussions to niche topics like permaculture or urban gardening. Joining these groups allows you to tap into a wealth of collective knowledge. You'll find posts about troubleshooting garden woes, exchanging DIY project tips, or simply sharing the joy of a successful harvest. Instagram, too, is a treasure trove of inspiration. By following popular homesteading hashtags, you can discover a stream of innovative ideas and beautiful snapshots from homesteaders who find creativity in every corner of their land. These visual stories not only motivate but also connect you to a wider community that shares your passions.

We love sharing our own homesteading journey on social media through **Homestead Mentors.** You can follow along with us and see what's happening around our homestead by searching for #**HomesteadMentors** on your favorite platforms. Whether it's a peek at our garden beds, our family milk cow, or tips for creating homemade remedies, we're always excited to share our experiences and connect with others who share our passion for sustainable living.

Online forums provide yet another avenue for engagement and learning. Platforms like Reddit and Permies offer spaces where homesteaders gather to discuss every facet of this lifestyle. These forums facilitate an exchange of experiences, troubleshooting advice, and practical tips. It's like sitting around a digital campfire, where seasoned homesteaders share their wisdom, and newcomers bring fresh perspectives and questions. The anonymity of forums often encourages open and honest discussions, making them a valuable resource for those seeking advice without the intimidation of face-to-face interactions. Here, you can ask questions ranging from crop rotation strategies to solar panel installation, knowing you're tapping into a diverse pool of expertise.

Building a personal online presence can also amplify your homesteading experience. Starting a blog or YouTube channel allows you to document and share your journey, creating a digital diary that others can follow and learn from. It's an opportunity to showcase your successes, reflect on challenges, and connect with a global audience who can relate to your experiences. Regular updates keep your followers engaged, offering them insights into your daily life, new projects, or tips you've found particularly useful. This ongoing dialogue enriches your network and builds a sense of community around your digital homestead, where ideas and encouragement flow freely.

However, as with any online interaction, maintaining positivity and respect is paramount. Establishing personal boundaries for social media use helps prevent burnout and ensures your interactions remain constructive. Decide how much time you want to spend online and what you're comfortable sharing about your life. Encouraging positive feedback and constructive criticism creates a supportive environment where everyone feels valued and heard. Remember, behind every screen is a person with their own story and challenges.

Treat each interaction with kindness and empathy, fostering a community that thrives on mutual respect and shared goals.

The digital world, with its endless connections and opportunities, is a vast landscape ready to be explored. By utilizing it thoughtfully, you can expand your homesteading network, drawing inspiration and support from a global community that shares your vision for a sustainable, self-sufficient life.

Sharing Resources and Knowledge

In the realm of homesteading, the concept of sharing extends beyond the exchange of ideas; it encompasses tangible resources that can ease the burdens of individual efforts.

Establishing a resource exchange system within your community can be a game-changer. Imagine an informal network where tools, seeds, and other resources circulate freely among neighbors and fellow homesteaders. Organizing tool-sharing schedules is a practical first step. This approach not only reduces the need for everyone to own every piece of equipment but also fosters trust and collaboration. For instance, you might borrow a tiller for your spring planting and lend a cider press in the fall. Such exchanges build a sense of community ownership and stewardship, reinforcing relationships and creating a supportive network.

Hosting seed swaps and plant exchanges can further enrich this resource-sharing model. These events allow homesteaders to share the abundance of their harvests, exchanging seeds for plants they may not have grown before. Picture a community gathering where tables overflow with jars of seeds and trays of seedlings, each with a story and a potential future. These swaps offer more than just practical benefits; they deepen the connection between participants, as each shared seed represents a piece of one's garden passed on to another. By encouraging diversity in your garden, you also contribute to the resilience and adaptability of your local ecosystem. Organizing these swaps can be as simple as designating a time and place, or as elaborate as themed events with workshops and guest speakers.

Beyond physical resources, the sharing of knowledge is a cornerstone of any thriving homesteading community. Documenting and sharing your expertise can empower others and reinforce your own skills. Consider writing guides or tutorials that outline specific skills you've mastered. Whether it's a step-by-step guide to building a compost bin or tips on fermenting vegetables, these resources can serve as valuable educational tools. For those who are more visually inclined, recording instructional videos can offer a dynamic way to share knowledge. These videos cater to visual learners who benefit from seeing processes in action. Platforms like YouTube or local community websites can host these resources, making them accessible to a wide audience.

The benefits of knowledge sharing extend far beyond the immediate impact. By fostering an environment where collaborative problem-solving is the norm, you create a community that is resilient and adaptable. Each shared solution or piece of advice strengthens the collective wisdom, offering diverse perspectives and approaches to common challenges. As you share your knowledge, you also build a reputation as a knowledgeable resource within the community. This recognition can lead to opportunities for further engagement, such as speaking at local events or being sought out for advice. The act of teaching others often reinforces your own understanding, deepening your mastery of the subject matter.

To formalize these knowledge-sharing efforts, consider creating structured learning opportunities, such as workshops or courses. This can start with developing a curriculum or lesson plan tailored to the interests and needs of your community. Workshops might range from introductory sessions on basic gardening techniques to advanced classes on renewable energy systems. Identifying potential guest speakers or instructors can enrich the learning experience, bringing in experts who can offer fresh insights and specialized knowledge. These events can be organized in collaboration with local organizations or as part of community festivals, further integrating homesteading into the cultural fabric of your area. By creating spaces for exchange and learning, you contribute to a culture of continuous growth and mutual support, where knowledge is valued and celebrated.

Hosting Community Workshops

Bringing people together to share skills and passion for homesteading can have a profound impact on both the individuals involved and the community at large. Planning and organizing a workshop begins with selecting topics that resonate with your community's interests. To identify these interests, chat with fellow homesteaders, survey potential attendees, or observe which topics generate excitement in local discussions. Once you have a topic, the next step is finding a suitable venue. This could be a community center, a local library, or even a spacious backyard. Ensure the space accommodates your expected number of participants comfortably, offering enough room for both demonstration and interaction. Consider accessibility when choosing your venue, as easy access encourages a diverse range of attendees. Collaborating with local organizations can also provide resources and establish credibility, helping your event reach a broader audience.

Keeping participants engaged is crucial for a successful workshop. People learn best when they're actively involved, so incorporate hands-on activities and demonstrations that allow them to practice new skills. Whether it's building a simple compost bin or preparing a homemade herbal remedy, these activities make the learning experience tangible and memorable. Encourage interaction and discussion by setting aside time for questions and group conversations. Create an open atmosphere where participants feel comfortable sharing their thoughts and experiences. This interaction enriches the learning process and fosters a sense of community among attendees. Consider inviting guest speakers or experts who can provide unique insights and answer questions from different perspectives.

Promotion plays a vital role in the success of your workshop. Utilize social media platforms to spread the word, creating event pages and sharing updates with your network. Local advertising can also be effective, especially when targeting those not as active online.

Distribute flyers at community hubs like farmer's markets, garden supply stores, and local cafes. Collaborating with libraries and community centers can further enhance your outreach. They often have bulletin boards or newsletters where you can advertise your event, reaching an audience already interested in community activities. Remember, clear and engaging communication about what participants will gain from attending your workshop can significantly boost interest and attendance.

Evaluating the success of your workshop is essential for planning future events. Distribute surveys to gather participant feedback, asking about their learning experience, suggestions for improvement, and topics they'd like to explore. This feedback provides valuable insights into what worked well and what could be enhanced. Reflect on your personal teaching experience, too-consider what felt effective and where you encountered challenges. These reflections help refine your approach, ensuring each subsequent workshop is an improvement over the last. You create a dynamic learning environment that evolves alongside your community's needs by continually assessing and adapting.

Hosting workshops not only empowers participants with new skills but also strengthens community bonds. As you plan these events, remember that the goal is to inspire and connect, creating a space where knowledge flows freely, and shared passions unite. Each workshop is a step toward a more informed, resilient, and cohesive community, one that supports its members in their homesteading endeavors. In the next chapter, we will explore ways to overcome common homesteading challenges, ensuring that the skills and connections developed in these workshops are put to effective use in building sustainable, fulfilling lives.

10

OVERCOMING COMMON
HOMESTEADING CHALLENGES

When I first embarked on my homesteading adventure, I was brimming with excitement and a bit of trepidation. The thought of cultivating a lifestyle grounded in self-sufficiency and sustainability was deeply appealing, yet l soon realized that managing time and resources effectively would be a crucial aspect of this journey. With countless tasks vying for attention, from tending the garden to preserving the harvest, it became evident that prioritizing was not just beneficial but essential. It's a balancing act that requires thoughtfulness and flexibility, allowing you to juggle the demands of homesteading with other aspects of life without losing your sanity.

One of the most valuable lessons I've learned is the power of creating daily and weekly task lists. By laying out your tasks in a clear, organized manner, you can visualize what needs to be accomplished and prioritize accordingly. Start each day by identifying high-impact activities that yield the best results, such as watering your plants or checking on the hens. These tasks form the backbone of your routine, ensuring that essential duties are not overlooked. It's important to remain realistic about what can be achieved in a day, allowing for unexpected interruptions and adjustments as needed. By focusing on the most crucial tasks, you can maintain productivity without feeling overwhelmed.

Technology can be a fantastic ally in streamlining homesteading activities. There are numerous apps available that can aid in task scheduling and reminders, making it easier to keep track of what needs to be done and when. For instance, you might use an app to set reminders for feeding the animals or for when to start your seeds indoors. Digital inventory tracking for supplies can also be a game-changer, helping you monitor your stock of seeds, animal feed, and other essentials. These tools free up mental space, allowing you to concentrate on the hands-on work that homesteading requires. According to an article on Homestead.org, apps like the Garden Time Planner provide region-specific gardening schedules, ensuring you plant at the optimal time for your area (Source 1).

Homesteading is often seen as a solitary pursuit but delegating and sharing responsibilities can significantly enhance your time management. Involving family members in specific homesteading tasks not only lightens the load but also fosters a sense of teamwork and shared accomplishment. Assign tasks based on individual strengths and interests; perhaps one person excels at building while another enjoys cooking. Establishing a community task exchange program can also be beneficial. By connecting with neighbors or fellow homesteaders, you can trade services and expertise, whether swapping gardening tips or lending a hand with livestock care. This collaborative approach not only optimizes efficiency but also strengthens community bonds.

Balancing homesteading with other commitments is another essential aspect of effective time management. Setting realistic time boundaries is crucial to prevent burnout. Allocate dedicated "homestead time" in your daily routine, like you would schedule any other important activity. This could be an hour in the morning before work or a couple of hours on the weekend. By carving out specific time slots for homesteading, you ensure it remains a priority without overshadowing other responsibilities. It's also important to be gentle with yourself and recognize that some days might not go as planned, and that's okay.

Flexibility and adaptability are your best allies in maintaining a healthy balance.

Interactive Element: Weekly Homesteading Planner

Create a simple planner to organize and prioritize your weekly homesteading tasks. Consider including sections for daily tasks, high-impact activities, and family or community involvement. Use this planner to reflect on your weekly progress and adjust as needed for the following week.

Incorporating these strategies into your homesteading routine can transform how you manage your time and resources. By prioritizing tasks, leveraging technology, and embracing collaboration, you create a more sustainable and enjoyable homesteading experience. This proactive approach not only enhances your productivity but also enriches your connection to the land and those who share it with you.

10.2 Adapting to Climate and Soil Changes

Understanding and adapting to climate and soil changes is an indispensable skill in homesteading. With weather patterns becoming increasingly unpredictable, it's vital to stay informed and flexible. Installing a small weather station can be a game-changer. This tool provides real-time data on temperature, humidity, and rainfall, helping you make informed decisions about your crops and livestock. If a weather station sounds too technical or costly, online resources and apps can also keep you updated on local forecasts and climate trends. Adjusting planting schedules based on this data ensures that your crops have the best chance of thriving. Planting too early might expose young seedlings to unexpected frosts, while planting too late can result in heat stress. By aligning your activities with the weather, you create a more resilient homestead that can better withstand the whims of Mother Nature.

Right after I had planted the garden after Mother's Day weekend, we had a late frost, and it killed all of my squash, tomatoes, cucumbers, and beans. I remember the sinking feeling in my stomach as I surveyed the damage, knowing how much effort had gone into those plants. Thankfully, I had anticipated this possibility and kept extra starts inside-just in case. Having those backup plants ready allowed me to replant quickly, and we were still able to save the crop. Over the years, I've learned to focus on plants that thrive in our unpredictable Wyoming climate. Carrots, potatoes, celery, broccolini, spinach, lettuce, sweet peas, and beans have become staples in our garden because they consistently produce well despite our colder growing season.

Soil health is the backbone of any successful gardening endeavor, and its importance cannot be overstated. To improve soil resilience against climate variability, consider incorporating organic matter and compost into your routine. These materials enhance soil structure, improve water retention, and provide essential nutrients that plants need to thrive. Regularly testing soil pH and nutrient levels helps you understand its current state and identify deficiencies. Home testing kits are a convenient option, but local agricultural extensions often provide more comprehensive testing services. With this information, you can tailor amendments to your soil's needs, ensuring it remains fertile and productive. A balanced soil pH, for instance, can enhance nutrient uptake and support healthy plant growth. By focusing on soil health, you lay the groundwork for a robust garden that can endure shifting climates.

Climate-responsive strategies are vital in adapting your homestead to environmental changes. During heatwaves, shade cloths can protect vulnerable plants from scorching sun rays. These lightweight fabrics, available in different densities, are draped over plants to reduce sunlight exposure and lower temperatures by several degrees. For livestock, offering shaded areas and ample water is essential to prevent heat stress. Additionally, building windbreaks can shield your garden and animals from harsh winds and storms.

Strategically planting trees or erecting fences can break the wind's force, reducing damage to plants and soil erosion. These measures are simple yet effective ways to enhance your homestead's resilience to climate extremes.

Microclimates, those small areas where conditions vary from the surrounding environment, offer unique opportunities for optimizing growing conditions. By understanding and utilizing microclimates, you can make the most of your available space. Planting sensitive crops in sheltered areas, such as near south-facing walls, can provide extra warmth and protection during cooler months. Alternatively, exploiting sunny spots for heat-loving plants like tomatoes or peppers can yield more abundant harvests.

Identifying these microclimates involves observing your homestead at different times of the day and year, noting areas that receive more sun, shade, or protection from wind. By strategically placing plants in these optimal spots, you create a diversified and productive homestead.

These strategies for adapting to climate and soil changes not only increase your homestead's productivity but also build resilience against the challenges posed by a changing environment. Each adjustment, from monitoring weather to enhancing soil health, contributes to a thriving ecosystem that supports both plants and animals.

Embracing these practices ensures that your homestead remains a vibrant and sustainable haven, regardless of what nature throws your way.

10.3 Dealing with Space Constraints

Indoor gardening is another brilliant approach. With the help of grow lights, even those without outdoor space can produce fresh food year-round. Windowsill gardens are a charming option for growing herbs like chives, mint, and basil, while grow lights can support crops like cherry tomatoes, microgreens, and lettuce indoors. I've been amazed by how I can turn a sunny kitchen corner into a thriving green space, ready for harvest whenever we need fresh ingredients.

The Magic of Microgreens

One of our favorite ways to keep fresh greens on the table all year, especially during the long Wyoming winters, is by growing microgreens indoors. These tiny but mighty plants are not only easy to grow but are also packed with nutrients. Microgreens are young vegetables harvested just after the first true leaves appear. Despite their small size, they contain a concentrated burst of vitamins, minerals, and antioxidants. Studies show that microgreens can have up to 40 times more nutrients than their mature counterparts!

We've grown everything from broccoli and radish microgreens to pea shoots and sunflower greens, and each variety brings its own unique flavor and health benefits. Broccoli microgreens, for example, are rich in sulforaphane, a powerful antioxidant linked to reducing inflammation and improving cellular health. Radish microgreens offer a spicy kick and are full of vitamin C and potassium. Pea shoots are crisp, sweet, and an excellent source of protein and fiber.

Growing microgreens indoors is incredibly simple and requires minimal space:

1. **Choose a shallow tray or container** with drainage holes.
2. **Fill it with a thin layer of high-quality potting soil** or a grow mat.
3. **Evenly scatter your seeds** (broccoli, radish, peas, or a microgreen mix).
4. **Mist the seeds with water** and cover them with another tray or cloth for the first few days to encourage germination.
5. **Once sprouted, expose them to light-a** sunny windowsill or a grow light works perfectly.

6. **Harvest them when they are 1-3 inches tall,** usually within 7-14 days, using scissors to snip them just above the soil.

These tiny greens are versatile in the kitchen. We love adding them to salads, sandwiches, soups, and even smoothies for an extra boost of nutrition. They're not just healthy-they're incredibly flavorful, elevating even the simplest meal.

Small Space, Big Potential

When it comes to selecting plants for small spaces, some varieties perform exceptionally well:

- **Herbs:** Basil, thyme, chives, mint, parsley, and oregano thrive in containers and windowsill gardens.
- **Leafy Greens:** Lettuce, spinach, kale, and Swiss chard grow quickly and don't require much space.
- **Compact Vegetables:** Cherry tomatoes, bush beans, radishes, dwarf carrots, and cucumbers (trained on a trellis) are excellent choices.
- **Fruits:** Strawberries grow beautifully in hanging baskets or stackable planters.
- **Microgreens:** Broccoli, radish, sunflower shoots, pea shoots, and mixed greens are perfect for small trays indoors.

It is crucial to think creatively about space utilization. Re-purposing old wooden crates as raised beds, transforming balcony railings into trellis systems, or using stackable bins for root vegetables can make all the difference. Even vertical structures like ladders or shelves can become homes for potted plants, maximizing every square inch like we talked about earlier.

This approach requires both adaptability and a willingness to experiment. It's about looking at every corner, windowsill, or balcony railing and seeing potential instead of limitations. Whether it's a few pots on a patio, a dedicated tray of microgreens indoors, or a fully stacked vertical garden, small spaces can yield an incredible abundance of herbs, vegetables, and fruits. Watching friends work magic in their compact spaces has reminded me that homesteading isn't defined by acreage-it's defined by intention, creativity, and care.

10.4 Navigating Financial Investments Wisely

When you first step into homesteading, the freedom and possibility are exhilarating. But like any new venture, it comes with its own set of financial hurdles. Creating and sticking to a budget is your roadmap to success. Start by categorizing expenses into essential and nonessential. Essentials might include seeds, feed, or basic tools-those things you absolutely can't do without. Non-essentials could be that fancy new garden gadget or extra decor for your chicken coop. By clearly defining these categories, you can decide where to allocate your resources. It's also wise to set aside funds for unexpected repairs or emergencies.

Whether it's a sudden storm damaging your greenhouse or an unforeseen veterinary bill, having a small cushion can alleviate stress and keep your projects on track.

Finding affordable supplies and materials is another cornerstone of budget-friendly homesteading. One of the best ways to save money is by purchasing second-hand tools and equipment. Thrift stores, garage sales, and online marketplaces can be treasure troves.

You'd be surprised at the quality and variety of items you can find if you keep an eye out. Another tip is to join local co-ops. These cooperatives often offer discounts on bulk purchases, from seeds and soil to feed and more. By pooling resources with other homesteaders, you can take advantage of these savings, allowing you to stretch your budget further than you might have thought possible.

Another valuable option, especially for those who may not have the financial means to purchase their own land right away, is to seek opportunities to help on someone else's farm or homestead. Many landowners have unused sections ofland or garden plots that they'd love to see cultivated but lack the time, energy, or resources to do it themselves. Offering to tend a section of their land in exchange for garden space can be a mutually beneficial arrangement. Not only does this provide you with an opportunity to grow your own food, but it also allows you to gain hands-on experience in farming or homesteading without the initial financial burden of property ownership.

Sometimes, these arrangements can grow into long-term opportunities, like renting a small piece ofland or partnering on larger homesteading projects. I've seen friends successfully grow an entire season's worth of produce on borrowed land, sharing a portion of the harvest with the landowner in gratitude. This type of arrangement builds trust, community, and resourcefulness-values at the very heart of homesteading. Whether you're helping a neighbor milk their cows, planting crops on borrowed land, or tending a community garden, these experiences provide invaluable knowledge and connections that will serve you well when the time comes to invest in your own property.

While these options are excellent starting points, investing in real estate can also provide long-term benefits when approached thoughtfully. When we lived in town, we bought a home that needed some fixing up. After about five years, we finished all of our projects on the home and yard and sold the house at a profit. With that profit, we were able to buy some land with another home already ready to live in. Since we've been on our homestead, we've seen its value grow steadily. At one point, we decided to take out a HELOC loan (Home Equity Line of Credit) to invest in another piece of property. Real estate in our area was becoming more expensive, and we saw an opportunity not only to secure a space for our parents but also to create a potential rental property in the future.

After a few years, we spoke with our parents and realized they wouldn't be comfortable in the townhome we had purchased because all the bedrooms were on the lower level. They felt it wasn't the right fit for them. Brett and I then had a long conversation about whether we should keep the townhome or sell it and reinvest the profit into our homestead.

Ultimately, we decided to sell the property and use the funds for projects that would directly benefit our homestead and improve our quality of life. Some of the things we have done and plan to do include:

- **Building a dry sauna and cold plunge for their health benefits.**
- **Replacing the worn-out white carpet in our home with durable flooring better suited to farm life.**
- **Constructing a new barn to create a rental space and offer a place for family and friends to stay when they visit.**

Currently, our camper serves as our guest space, but having a dedicated barn-style guest space will be a game-changer for us.

Another investment we made was in our tractor. It was one of the largest single purchases we've made for our homestead, but like I said earlier, it has been worth every penny. The tractor has allowed us to complete projects efficiently that would have been nearly impossible by hand. Best of all, we were able to secure an interest-free loan for it, making the financial burden more manageable. Sometimes, an upfront investment in quality equipment pays off tenfold in time, labor savings, and productivity.

Each decision was carefully considered, and we've always tried to remain debt-free or pay off any debts as quickly as possible. Homesteading requires patience and a willingness to take calculated financial risks, but when done wisely, those investments can truly transform your life.

Evaluating cost-benefit ratios is crucial when deciding where to invest your hard-earned money. This means weighing the potential return on investment (ROI) against the upfront costs. For instance, installing solar panels may have a significant initial expense, but over time, the savings on energy bills can make it a worthwhile investment. Similarly, compare the costs of DIY projects to purchased solutions. Sometimes, building a compost bin from reclaimed wood can be cheaper and more satisfying than buying a pre-made one. On other occasions, investing in a high-quality tool might save you money in the long run, avoiding the cost and hassle of frequent replacements.

Exploring alternative financing options can open doors to opportunities that might otherwise seem out of reach. Grants and subsidies for sustainable practices are available through various organizations, including government programs and non-profits. These funds can help cover costs for energy-efficient upgrades, organic certification, or even educational workshops. Take the time to research and apply for these opportunities.

Crowdfunding is another avenue to consider, particularly for larger projects. Platforms like Kickstarter or GoFundMe allow you to share your vision with a broader audience, inviting them to support your homesteading dreams. This approach not only raises funds but also builds a community around your project, creating a network of supporters invested in your success.

The financial aspect of homesteading can feel daunting, but with careful planning and a touch of creativity, you can navigate it successfully. By budgeting wisely, sourcing supplies affordably, assessing investments critically, and exploring alternative funding, you can cultivate a homestead that reflects both your values and your financial reality. As you grow in this lifestyle, these strategies will become second nature, empowering you to make choices that sustain your homestead for the long haul.

In this chapter, we've explored practical ways to manage time, adapt to environmental changes, and make wise financial choices in homesteading. These skills are the foundation of a resilient and thriving homestead. As you continue to cultivate your space, remember that each challenge is an opportunity for growth and innovation. This mindset will carry you forward as we move to the next chapter, where we'll delve into sustaining motivation and cultivating resilience in your homesteading endeavors.

11

SUSTAINING MOTIVATION AND CULTIVATING RESILIENCE

Imagine waking up to the sound of birdsong, the sun casting a warm glow over your garden. Your morning coffee tastes richer because the milk came from your own goats, the honey from your bees. You feel a sense of fulfillment, yet there's a plan to tackle-the goals you set for your homestead. Setting goals can be the compass that guides your homesteading journey, helping you maintain direction and motivation. But to keep that flame burning, these goals must be realistic and achievable. It's all too easy to dream big and then get overwhelmed. Recognizing what you can truly accomplish with the resources at hand is crucial. This might mean focusing on short-term goals, like planting a new herb garden, while keeping an eye on long-term aspirations, like achieving full energy independence with solar panels.

Creating a goal-setting framework can transform these dreams into actionable steps. A structured approach ensures your aspirations don't remain distant stars but become reachable milestones. The SMART criteria-Specific, Measurable, Achievable, Relevant, and Time-bound-serve as a practical guideline. For example, instead of a vague goal like "grow more vegetables," aim for "plant and maintain a 10-square-foot vegetable garden by the end of spring." Writing down these goals in a dedicated journal or crafting a vision board can be incredibly empowering. Seeing your dreams visualized can ignite the drive to make them a reality, while the act of crossing off completed tasks brings unparalleled satisfaction.

As life unfolds, it's natural for goals to shift. Flexibility is key. Regularly revisiting and adjusting your goals allows you to adapt to new circumstances or interests. Perhaps a new job has limited your time, or a newfound passion for herbal remedies demands attention. Quarterly or annual evaluations of your goals ensure they align with your current situation. Incremental adjustments based on progress keep your journey dynamic and responsive rather than rigid and exhausting. This adaptability helps you stay motivated, as each goal feels attainable and relevant.

Finally, celebrating milestones and achievements is essential for maintaining motivation. Homesteading is hard work, and recognizing your progress is vital. Host small celebrations for reaching significant goals, like finally harvesting those heirloom tomatoes or constructing a new chicken coop. Invite friends and family to share in your accomplishments or simply take a moment to reflect on your personal growth. Such celebrations not only fuel your determination but also reinforce the rewarding nature of your homesteading efforts.

Milestone Reflection Section

Set aside time each month to reflect on what you've accomplished. Write down three achievements you're proud of and consider how they contribute to your larger goals. Reflect on the lessons learned and how they may shape your future plans. This practice not only acknowledges your hard work but also inspires continued progress and resilience in your homesteading journey.

11.2 Learning from Failures and Setbacks

In the world of homesteading, not everything will go according to plan. That's a given. But here's the thing: every misstep is a chance to learn and grow. Adopting a growth mindset means viewing failures not as roadblocks but as feedback. It's about understanding that when your seedlings fail to sprout, or your DIY project goes awry, these aren't the end of the world. They're lessons. Instead of beating yourself up, consider what went wrong with curiosity and openness. Did you plant too early? Was there a step missed? By analyzing these moments without self-criticism, you equip yourself to avoid similar pitfalls in the future.

Patterns often emerge from these experiences. By keeping a failure log, you can start identifying recurring challenges. This simple act of writing things down-what happened, why, and what you did-can reveal areas that need more attention or a different approach. Maybe you notice that your soil needs more amendments or your time management needs tweaking. Once you know the patterns, brainstorming solutions becomes easier. Perhaps you need to change your watering schedule, or maybe it's time to consult a pest control expert. Each solution you identify is another step towards refining your homesteading skills.

Overcoming setbacks is about building resilience. Each hurdle you clear strengthens your determination and patience. Remember the first time you tried baking bread and it came out like a brick? With each loaf, you learned a little more. You adjusted, persisted, and eventually, you got it right. It's the same with homesteading. Drawing lessons from past experiences helps cultivate patience, teaching you that persistence pays off. Over time, you'll find that these challenges are not just obstacles but opportunities to deepen your understanding and hone your skills.

Support and encouragement from others can be invaluable in this process. Whether it's joining a local support group or an online forum, connecting with others who share your passions can provide much-needed perspective and advice. Finding a mentor-someone who's been through the trials and triumphs-can offer personalized guidance that books and articles can't. Their insights and moral support can help you navigate the complexities of homesteading with more confidence.

11.3 Staying Inspired Through Success Stories

Sometimes, it's the stories of others that light the path forward. When you read about someone who turned a barren plot into a thriving oasis or watch a documentary about sustainable living, it's not just information-it's inspiration. These narratives remind you that the challenges you face are surmountable. They show you that resilience and creativity can cultivate a life full of abundance and joy. Biographies of renowned homesteaders are treasure troves of wisdom. They reveal the trials and triumphs of those who've walked the path before you. Documentaries offer visual journeys into the possibilities of sustainable living, sparking ideas you might not have considered.

Connecting with inspirational figures can also be a powerful motivator. Attend talks or workshops where experts share their insights and experiences. Listening to someone who has mastered a skill or overcome a significant hurdle can fuel your own determination.

Social media, too, can be a source of encouragement. Follow homesteaders who share their daily victories and setbacks. Their posts can serve as a reminder that you're not alone, that there's a community cheering you on, offering tips and encouragement from their own experiences.

Documenting your own successes can be equally inspiring, not just for you but for others. Keep a journal where you record the small victories and the lessons learned. Snap photos of your garden in full bloom or your latest DIY project. Reflecting on these moments of success helps cement them in your memory, reminding you of how far you've come.

Sharing these stories with others, whether through a blog, social media, or a simple conversation, spreads inspiration.

Your journey can motivate someone else to take that first step toward their dreams.

Creating a network of inspiration amplifies these efforts. Organize local meetups with like minded individuals where you can share experiences, swap tips, and celebrate each other's accomplishments. Online forums are another venue where success stories flourish. Here, you can exchange stories with people from all corners of the globe, each bringing their unique perspective and solution to the table. This sense of community can be a wellspring of support and motivation, reminding you that together, we're capable of remarkable things.

Embracing Continuous Learning

In the world of homesteading, the act of learning never truly ends. Each day brings a new challenge or opportunity, and whether it's plant you've never grown or a technique you've yet to try. Committing to lifelong learning keeps your mind agile and your homestead flourishing. Staying updated on new homesteading techniques is essential.

Innovations in sustainable practices and permaculture principles can offer fresh perspectives and solutions. But don't limit yourself to just homesteading topics. Exploring diverse subjects like carpentry or herbal medicine can complement your skills and open new doors. You might discover a passion for beekeeping or find joy in crafting natural remedies. Each new skill not only enhances your self-sufficiency but also enriches your life.

Exploring new skills can be an adventure in itself. Trying your hand at unfamiliar crafts or recipes expands your abilities and keeps the homesteading experience exciting. Perhaps you've always wanted to learn how to make cheese or build a birdhouse. Attending workshops or taking online courses can provide the guidance and inspiration you need.

These learning experiences often connect you with others who share your interests, fostering a sense of community and support. Embrace the opportunity to step outside your comfort zone. The skills you acquire can lead to new projects and possibilities, making your homestead even more rewarding.

To make the most of these learning opportunities, leverage the educational resources at your disposal. The internet is a treasure trove of tutorials and webinars that cater to every level of expertise. If you're a visual learner, video tutorials can be particularly helpful, breaking down complex tasks into manageable steps. Libraries are also invaluable, offering a wealth of books and materials on topics from organic gardening to renewable energy.

These resources provide a solid foundation for your continued education, allowing you to build knowledge at your own pace.

Reflecting on what you've learned is crucial for solidifying knowledge and gaining insights. Writing learning summaries helps you process information and track your progress.

Creating mind maps can visually organize your thoughts, revealing connections between

different concepts. Discussing new insights with peers or mentors can deepen your understanding and offer fresh perspectives. By regularly reflecting on your experiences, you'll not only retain more information but also develop a clearer vision for your homesteading goals.

Balancing Homesteading with Modern Life

In the midst of all the homesteading excitement, there's the reality of balancing it with the demands of modern life. It's about weaving those homesteading tasks into the fabric of your daily routine without feeling overwhelmed. One way to do this is by scheduling homesteading activities around your work commitments. For instance, you might reserve simpler tasks, like watering the garden or feeding the chickens, for weekday mornings before heading to work. Save the more time-intensive projects, such as building a new compost bin or preserving a batch of homemade jam, for the weekends when you can fully immerse yourself in the activity without the rush. This approach ensures you're consistently making progress without sacrificing your other responsibilities.

A healthy work-life balance is crucial, especially when your passions and responsibilities intersect. Setting boundaries is key to preventing overcommitment, which can lead to burnout. It's important to recognize when to say no, even to the projects you're passionate about, to maintain your mental and physical health. Prioritizing self-care alongside your homesteading tasks means knowing when to take a break and recharge. Whether it's an afternoon spent reading in the garden or a walk through the woods, these moments help keep your energy and enthusiasm intact. After all, you can't pour from an empty cup, and a well-rested homesteader is a more effective one.

Technology can be a wonderful ally in achieving this balance. Smart home devices, like programmable thermostats or automated irrigation systems, can handle routine tasks, giving you more freedom. Task management apps can help organize your day, sending reminders for everything from sowing seeds to checking beehives. These tools allow you to focus on the more rewarding aspects of homesteading without getting bogged down by the minutiae. By delegating some of the workload to technology, you free up time to enjoy the fruits of your labor-whether savoring a meal made with your own produce or crafting with homegrown herbs.

Embracing flexibility is another cornerstone of balancing homesteading with life's unpredictability. Plans can change, and that's perfectly okay. Being adaptable means adjusting your plans without feeling guilty. Some days, the energy and motivation might not be there, and that's normal. Recognizing the ebb and flow of motivation allows you to be kinder to yourself. It's about listening to what you need and adapting your activities accordingly. By doing so, you maintain a sustainable pace that respects both your ambitions and well-being.

11.6 Exploring Minimalism in Homesteading

Modern life often feels like a race, with too many things competing for our attention and space. Embracing minimalism within a homesteading lifestyle offers a chance to slow down and focus on what truly matters. It's about stripping away the excess and honing in on the essentials. This approach doesn't mean you live with nothing; instead, it's an invitation to prioritize quality over quantity in both tools and resources. Choosing a few high-quality, multifunctional tools can often serve you better than a cluttered shed full of gadgets you rarely use. This simplicity lets you focus on the meaningful pursuits that drew you to homesteading in the first place, like growing your own food or crafting with your hands.

Decluttering is a practical first step towards minimalism. Regularly assess your spaces, identifying items that no longer serve a purpose. This could be the gardening tool that's seen better days, or the cluttered pantry filled with expired goods. By conducting regular decluttering sessions, you create a more efficient and enjoyable work environment.

Consider using storage solutions like labeled bins or pegboards to keep your homestead organized. A well-ordered space not only improves productivity but also brings a sense of calm, making daily tasks feel more manageable and less overwhelming.

Moving towards a minimalist mindset encourages a shift in values, placing emphasis on experiences and relationships rather than material possessions. Practicing gratitude for what you already own helps reduce the impulse to constantly acquire more. It's about finding satisfaction in what you have, not what you lack. As you become more mindful of your consumption, you'll likely find your life feels fuller, not emptier. This mindset shift can be incredibly liberating, allowing you to focus on the joys of homesteading without the constant pressure to keep up with consumer trends.

Balancing minimalism with the practical needs of home-steading requires discernment. Identify what is essential and what is not. Consider creating multifunctional spaces where a single area serves multiple purposes, like a workshop that doubles as a storage area or a kitchen garden that also provides herbs for natural remedies. This thoughtful approach ensures that minimalism enhances rather than hinders your homesteading efforts, creating a harmonious environment that supports both simplicity and self-sufficiency.

Utilizing Technology Without Overwhelm

In today's tech-driven world, finding the right tools can enhance your homesteading life without adding unnecessary complexity. It's about choosing technology that addresses your specific needs, whether it's a smart irrigation system to automate watering or a solar charger for your off-grid adventures. Start by identifying the areas in your homestead that could benefit from technological assistance, like energy management or task scheduling.

Avoid the temptation to clutter your life with gadgets that promise more than they deliver. Instead, focus on tools that genuinely simplify your workload and support your goals, ensuring they integrate seamlessly into your daily routines without overshadowing the hands-on joy that homesteading brings.

Setting boundaries for technology use is crucial to preventing it from becoming a source of stress rather than support. Designate tech-free times or zones in your home where devices are off-limits, allowing you to engage fully with your environment and loved ones. Regular digital detoxes, where you step away from screens and immerse yourself in the tangible world, can rejuvenate your mind and spirit. These practices help maintain a healthy balance, ensuring that technology serves as a tool rather than a tether, keeping your focus on the present moment and the tasks at hand. They also foster a sense of peace, allowing you to appreciate the simplicity and beauty of your natural surroundings.

Technology also offers incredible opportunities for learning and inspiration. Online courses and tutorials provide access to a wealth of knowledge, allowing you to explore new skills from the comfort of your home. Following homesteading influencers on social media can spark ideas and offer solutions to common challenges, connecting you with a broader community of like-minded individuals. These platforms can be a source of motivation, revealing innovative techniques and fostering a sense of camaraderie among those who share your passion. They remind you that you're part of a larger movement, one that values sustainability and self-sufficiency in a rapidly changing world.

Maintaining a tech-life balance is about integrating technology into your homesteading activities without letting it overshadow the tangible experiences that bring fulfillment. Engage in hands-on projects-whether it's planting a new garden bed or crafting homemade soap-without the distractions of digital devices. Incorporate mindful tech practices into your routine, using technology as a complement to, rather than a replacement for, the rich, sensory experiences of homesteading. This balance allows you to enjoy the best of both worlds, harnessing the benefits of modern tools while staying grounded in the simplicity and satisfaction of creating with your own hands.

Celebrating Your Homesteading Achievements

Acknowledging the milestones you've reached in your homesteading efforts is more than just a pat on the back-it's a vital part of sustaining your enthusiasm and commitment.

Imagine creating a visual timeline of your accomplishments, from your first successful harvest to the DIY projects that now enhance your living space. This timeline becomes a tapestry of your hard work, a testament to your dedication and growth. Sharing these achievements with friends and family not only spreads joy but also encourages others to appreciate the rewarding journey of self-sufficiency. It's not just about the destination but the steps that got you there, each one deserving of recognition.

Establishing personal traditions or rituals around your homesteading lifestyle can add depth and meaning to your everyday activities. Hosting seasonal feasts with produce from your own garden is a wonderful way to celebrate the changing seasons and the fruits of your labor. These gatherings become cherished events, where the table is filled with homemade dishes and the air with laughter and stories. Annual reflection practices, where you take time to look back on the year's challenges and triumphs, can also be incredibly fulfilling. These rituals ground your homesteading efforts in a sense of purpose, connecting you to the rhythms of nature and the cycles of growth and rest.

Documenting your homesteading experiences is another powerful way to celebrate your progress. Keeping a detailed journal allows you to capture the nuances of your daily activities, from the first seedlings sprouting to the lessons learned from a failed crop.

Creating a photo album or scrapbook can visually showcase the transformation of your homestead over time. These records not only serve as a source of inspiration for the future but also as a reminder of how much you've achieved. They offer a tangible way to revisit your journey, reflecting on the evolution of both you and your homestead.

Sharing your homesteading journey with a broader community can be incredibly rewarding. Writing blog posts or articles about your experiences allows you to offer insights and inspiration to others who may be just starting out or facing similar challenges. Hosting open house events for fellow homesteaders can create opportunities for knowledge exchange and community building. These interactions foster a sense of belonging and shared purpose, reminding you that you're part of a larger movement toward sustainable living. By sharing your knowledge and experiences, you contribute to the collective wisdom of the homesteading community, encouraging others to embark on their own paths to self-sufficiency and resilience.

CONCLUSION

As we come to the end of this journey together, I hope you feel as excited and inspired as I do about the path that lies ahead. We've explored a world where homesteading isn't just a lifestyle-it's a way to connect deeply with the earth and our communities. You now hold a toolkit filled with ideas and strategies to create your own version of homesteading, whether you're on a sprawling rural property or in an urban apartment with just a tiny balcony to call your garden.

Throughout these chapters, we've delved into themes that are close to my heart, like the beautiful harmony between modern technology and time-tested traditions. We've seen how sustainability is not just a buzzword but a meaningful way to live, offering us healthier foods and a smaller footprint on our planet. We've also talked about the significance of community-how sharing resources and experiences can enrich our journey and make it more rewarding.

Homesteading is deeply personal, yet it's also wonderfully adaptable. It's about taking ideas and making them your own, fitting them into your life in ways that work for you. Whether you're starting with a small herb garden on your windowsill or diving into raising chickens, the key is to begin with where you are and what you have. This book was written to empower you, to show you that no matter your starting point, you can create a thriving, self-sufficient space that reflects your values and dreams.

Also, remember that you're not alone on this journey. One of the most powerful aspects of homesteading is the community that comes with it. Whether you're connecting with local groups or engaging with fellow enthusiasts online, these connections can offer support, advice, and friendship. They remind us that while we strive for independence, community is what truly enriches our lives and our work

The adventure doesn't stop here. Keep learning, keep experimenting. Each season brings new opportunities and challenges. Whether it's trying out a new canning recipe or exploring renewable energy solutions, let curiosity be your guide. Homesteading is a lifelong journey of growth and discovery.

I invite you to take the next step, whatever that looks like for you. Plant that first seed, reach out to a fellow homesteader, or start a new project you've been dreaming about. Every small action brings you closer to the life you envision.

Reflecting on my own experiences, I remember the nervous excitement of our first days on the homestead. There were moments of doubt, but they were always overshadowed by the joy of each little success. The first eggs from our chickens, the first jar of homemade jam-it was all worth it. I want you to feel that same joy and fulfillment. Know that I am cheering you on every step of the way.

Thank you for choosing to explore homesteading with me. It's been an honor to share this journey with you. I hope this book has been a valuable companion, offering guidance and inspiration as you embark on your own path.

Looking to the future, I feel optimistic. With each person who embraces sustainable living, we move closer to a world that's kinder to our planet and to each other. Let's continue to cultivate independence, resilience, and a deeper connection to the environment. Together, we can sow the seeds for a brighter, more sustainable future.

REFERENCES

- *Mission/Vision statement? (homestead forum at permies)*
  https://permies.com/t/165514/Mission-Vision-statement
- *6 Steps to Financial Self Sufficiency for Homesteaders*
  https://homesteadlaunch.com/financial-self-sufficiency/
- *10 Gardening and Plant Recognition Apps Needs in 2023*
  https://www.techgadgetscanada.com/10-gardening-and-plant-recognition-apps that-every-green-thumb-needs/
- *How to Organize Your Homestead with a Planner*
  https://www.theprairiehomestead.com/2021/10/how-to-organize-your homestead-with-a-planner.html
- *Vertical vegetable garden ideas perfect for small spaces*
  https://www.wkrg.com/news/vertical-vegetable-garden-ideas-perfect-for-small spaces/
- *Urban Beekeeping Laws: Navigating City Regulations for ...*
  https://green beekeeping.com/city-beekeeping-legal-requirements/
- *Affordable Container Farms: Cost-Effective Solutions for ...* https://www.opticlimatefarm.com/a-news-affordable-container-farms-cost effective-solutions-for-sustainable-agriculture
- *Designing Polycultures for the Garden*
  http://www.hort.cornell.edu/brewer/polycultures / Polyculture%20Design%2Oslid es.pdf

- *Heirloom Gardening for Biodiversity* https://www.southernexposure.com/heirloom gardening-for-biodiversity/#:~:text=Genetic%20Diversity,plant%20diseases%20or%20other%2 0threats.
- *Climate-Smart Gardening* https://nj climateresourcecenter.rutgers.edu/climate_change_101/ climate-smart gardening/
- *Tipsheet: Organic Pest Management* https://www.ams.usda.gov/sites/default/files/media/Organic%20 Pest%20Manage ment_FINAL.pdf
- *The Ultimate Guide to Growing More Food in a Small Space* https://www.theseasonalhomestead.com/the-ultimate-guide-to-growing-more food-in-a-small-space/
- *Best Chicken Breeds For City Living* https://insteading.com/blog/best-chicken breeds/
- *DIY Chicken Coop Plans: 40+ Free Beginner ...* https://easycoops.com/
- *Beekeeping equipment - Mid-Atlantic Apiculture Research ...*
- https://canr.udel.edu/maarec/beekeeping-equipment/
- *An ethical foundation for careful animal husbandry* https://www.sciencedirect.com/science/article/pii/S1573521413000171
- *Lacto-Fermentation: How Does It Work?* https://www.thespruceeats.com/how lacto-fermentation-works-1327598
- *National Center for Home Food Preservation: Home Page* https://nchfp.uga.edu/
- *Conventional And Advanced Food-Drying Technology* http://www.ijstr.org/final print/jan2 021/Conventional-And-Advanced-Food-drying-Technology-A-Current Review.pdf
- *Causes and Possible Solutions for Problems with Canned Food* https://nchfp.uga.edu/how/can/general-information/causes-and-possible solutions-for-problems-with-canned-food/

References

- *DIY Solar Panel Installation: Step by Step Guide*
  https://www.gogreensolar.com/pages/diy-solar-installation-guide
- *What materials are used to make wind turbines?*
  https://www.vvcresources.com/what-materials-are-used-to-make-wind-turbines
- *The Complete Beginner's Guide to Greywater Systems*
  https://elemental.green/complete-beginner-guide-to-greywater-systems/
- *Off grid Solar System Components: what do you need?*
  https://sinovoltaics.com/learning-center/off-grid/off-grid-solar-system components/
- *Easy Beginner Woodworking Projects*
  https://www.familyhandyman.com/list/surprisingly-simple-woodworking projects-for-beginners/?srsltid=AfmBOoptoTMwOXIYEEiHgLFsw2S6UlgC1i0qnnFjuMqDp2mmd D4oEctc
- *9 Simple Herbal Remedies from Your Garden - Healthline*
  https://www.healthline.com/health/herbal-remedies-from-your-garden
- *65 Useful and Easy Upcycling Ideas for Every Skill Level*
  https://www.goodhousekeeping.com/home/craft-ideas/how-to/gl 39/ genius upcycling-ideas/
- *How To Make Natural Soap Using Gorgeous Organic ...*
  https://www.savvyhomemade.com/natural-organic-soap-recipes/
- *Home Grown Nutrition - Dr Earth* https://drearth.com/resources/article/home grown nutrition/#:~:text=Nutrient%20 Density,flavonoids)%2C%20micronutrients%20an d%20minerals.
- *The Benefits of Seasonal Eating: Fresh, Nutrient-Dense, and ...*
  https://hgic.clemson.edu/the-benefits-of-seasonal-eating-fresh-nutrient-dense and-budget-friendly/
- *Gardening as a Mindfulness Practice/ NC State Extension*
  https://extensiongardener.ces.ncsu.edu/2024/07/gardening-as-a-mindfulness practice/

- *67 Recipes to Make with Fresh Herbs* https://www. tasteofhome.com/collection/recipes-with-fresh herbs/?srsltid=AfmBOopBll66lEp71HT9qB_ aGxl8Z1rb6utOi_xOS7MWxpFQbr1D_Jq y
- *Find Your Homesteading Community: Your People are Out ...* https://www.homestead.org/lifestyle/finding-community-on-the-homestead/
- *Start a Homesteading Club* https://www. motherearthnews.com/homesteading-and livestock/ start-homesteading-club-zm0z2002znad/
- *How To Use Social Media To Promote Your Farm or ...* https://morningchores.com/how-to-promote-your-farm-or-homestead-on-social media/
- *7 Essential Tips for Hosting a Homesteading Workshop* https://farmwhereyoulive.com/7-essential-tips-for-hosting-a-homesteading workshop/
- *Helpful Homesteading Apps* https://www.homestead. org/lifestyle/helpful homesteading-apps/
- *How to Create a Better Microclimate in Your Garden* https://www.treehugger.com/how-create-better-microclimate-garden-6950904
- *The Ultimate Guide To Homesteading On A Budget* https://gubbahomestead.com/homesteading/the-ultimate-guide-to-homesteading on-a-budget/
- *Grants and Loans/ USDA* https://www.usda.gov/ topics/farming/grants-and-loans
- *How to Set Realistic Goals for Your Homestead and ...* https://www.oakhillhomestead.com/2018/ 12/ setting-realistic-goals-for-new year.html
- *Mindset of Learning and Growing - Sweet Momma's Farm* https://sweetmommasfarm.com/1/homesteading-is-a-mindset-of-learning-and growing/
- *The Benefits of Minimalist Homesteading* https://www. imperfectlyhappy.com/the benefits-of-minimalist-homesteading/

References

- *How Homesteaders Are Using High Tech to Save Energy* https://www.grit.com/tools/technology/modern-homesteading-how homesteaders-using-tech-to-save-energy-zbOz1905/

Keeping the Game Alive

Now that you hopefully have everything you need to achieve sustainable homesteading, it's time to pass on your newfound knowledge and show other readers where they can find the same help.

Please leave your honest opinion of this book on Amazon, you'll show other aspiring homesteaders where they can find the information they're looking for, and pass their passion for sustainable living forward.

Thank you for your help. Sustainable living is kept alive when we pass on our knowledge—and you're helping us to do just that.

Please Scan the QR Code Below to Leave a Review